Critical Guides to S

71 Julio Medem

Critical Guides to Spanish and Latin American Texts and Films

EDITED BY ALAN DEYERMOND & STEPHEN HART

JULIO MEDEM

Jo Evans

Lecturer in Spanish
University College London

London
Grant & Cutler Ltd 2007

ISBN: 978 0 7293 0451 1

Depósito legal: V. 4.929 - 2007

Printed in Spain by
Artes Gráficas Soler, S.L., Valencia
for
GRANT & CUTLER LTD
55–57 GREAT MARLBOROUGH STREET, LONDON W1F 7AY

Contents

For David and Marie

Acknowledgements

I would like to thank staff and students at the Department of Spanish and Latin American Studies, University College London for providing a rich and stimulating environment to work in over the last ten years. I have been lucky enough to work with many wonderful colleagues and students at UCL and would like to convey my particular gratitude to Stephen Hart, Claire Lindsay, Lee Grieveson and Claire Thompson.

I am much indebted to Núria Triana-Toribio for putting me in contact with Javier Herrera at the *Filmoteca Española*, who sourced material and provided access to many of the press articles referred to in this study: my thanks to you both. Members of my family also provided encouragement; my parents not only watched the films and pointed out potential new readings, but painstakingly proof-read drafts. Mistakes made in the final revisions will be mine and not theirs.

I am very grateful to Rob Stone who sent me a copy of his book on Medem, which was in press at the time of writing. This, I can thoroughly recommend to anyone interested in knowing more about Medem and the films, as well as cast and crew members. Thanks also to Antonio Sánchez for sending me at such short notice a copy of his article on women in *Vacas* and *La ardilla roja*. Many other colleagues, some known to me some not, have published work on Medem that has contributed to my own interpretations here. Their work is listed in full in the bibliography, but I would like to thank Isabel Santaolalla, Xon de Ros and Ann White in particular.

Some of the material used in chapters 2 and 3 has appeared elsewhere and I am grateful to publishers, Peter Lang and Intellect for permission to reprint here.

I should also like to thank Julio Medem, Cecilia Roca, Silvia Gómez at *Alicia Produce*, and Sophie MacMahon at *Sogecine* for kindly authorising the images used here, and publishers Peter Lang and Intellect for permission to reprint material first published in the following articles:

Evans, Jo, '*La ardilla roja*: the Compulsive Nostalgia of Popular Love Songs', in *Cultura Popular: Studies in Spanish and Latin American Popular Culture*, eds Shelly Godsland and Anne M. White (Oxford: Peter Lang, 2002), pp.147–162.

Evans, Jo, '*La madre muerta* (1993) and *Tierra* (1995): Basque Identity, or just the Other?', *Studies in European Cinema*, 4, 3 (2006), 173–183.

Introduction. Video Diaries/Celluloid Selves

'¿Qué hay al otro lado del agujero?'
'What's on the other side of the hole?'

Death Threats and Standing Ovations

In 1991, thirty-three year old Julio Medem was a little known Spanish director living on a Basque hillside. He was writing short stories and looking after his son while his wife worked. The couple both studied medicine, but Medem had given up the idea of becoming a psychiatrist to try and make a living as a film director. After a few successful short films his career had come to a standstill (*61*, p.160–161). Four years later, he was living in central Madrid, the famously reclusive Stanley Kubrick was trying to arrange a meeting and Steven Spielberg was hoping he would direct *Zorro* (*27*, p.16). By 2003, he had finished his sixth full-length film and was the focus of a national controversy and the object of death threats and standing ovations (*27*, p.16; *44*, p.283).

This introduction to Medem's work examines the first four feature films that influenced his flight from obscurity to notoriety, *Vacas* (*Cows*, 1992), *La ardilla roja* (*The Red Squirrel*, 1993), *Tierra* (*Earth*, 1996), and *Los amantes del Círculo Polar* (*Lovers of the Arctic Circle*, 1998). It will focus on the recurring themes and obsessions that have made Medem one of Spain's most highly regarded auteurs. Filming is a collaborative art and Medem has had the good fortune to work with the stars of the Spanish film industry, including cinematographer Javier Aguirresarobe and musician Alberto Iglesias. At the same time his films are clearly driven by an extraordinarily personal vision. He is always quick to acknowledge a debt to financial backing from Sogecine that allowed him to direct the kind of films that inspired one reviewer to call him 'cinema's last full-blown symbolist' (*36*, p.48). The four films examined in detail here were followed by *Lucía y el sexo* (*Sex and Lucia*, 2001) and the controversial documentary *La pelota vasca: La piel contra la piedra* (*Basque Ball: Skin Against Stone*, 2003). At the time of writing, his on-going exploration of the human psyche has led to the production of a documentary on schizophrenia, *Uno por ciento, esquizofrenia* (*One per cent, schizophrenia*), written and directed by Ione Hernández, and his next fiction film, *Caótica Ana* (Chaotic Ana) is said to be in post-production.

Contradictory responses divide his critics into 'admiradores y hostiles' (*37*, p.19) and one critic claims his films either bewitch or repel their viewers (*35*, p.82). The death threats and standing ovations were the result of the documentary he made on the subject of ETA terrorism. However, violently opposed critical reaction has always been a factor to which he says international success has gradually immunized him (*27*, p.16) and also helped overcome the vestiges of a childhood shyness he describes as 'casi enfermiza' ('almost unhealthy') (*3*, p.552).

Basque Origins and the Spanish 'New Wave'

In addition to shyness and critical conflict, Medem had to contend with controversial reactions to his geographical origins (*44*, p.219). He was born in San Sebastián in the Basque Country in 1958, so his films have been linked to what José Enrique Monterde calls 'a small avalanche' of Basque film from the 1980s that became 'one of the "spearheads" of Spanish film industry' (*41*, p.186). The early 1990s were disappointing years for Spanish film. During the 1980s and 90s, Barry Jordan and Rikki Morgan-Tamosunas note 'numerous instances of significant national and international success but against a background of industrial weakness and apparent long-term decline' (*41*, p.205). In the context of this decline, Medem is among the directors who inspired a new sense of hope (*38*, pp.29–30). The success of those born in the Basque country drew attention to the complications of the label 'Basque film'. These arose from the fact that Basque identity has been suppressed by the Spanish State and that directors such as Medem tended to avoid the label and to film, for financial reasons, in Castilian; although the success of Altuna and Esnal's Basque-language comedy, *¡Aupa Etxebeste!* (*Hi, Etxebeste!* 2005) is a hopeful sign for future Basque film-makers and producers.[1] In her article on *Vacas*, Xon de Ros concludes that 'since 1990 new Basque film-makers such as Medem have gained a central position in the Spanish film-market. However, the use of the label 'New Basque Cinema' for their work has become if anything constricting and misleading' (*48*, p.233). Clearly, there are on-going problems with the label, as Paul Julian Smith (59) and Isabel Santaolalla (57) have also noted, and perhaps it is because of this that wider questions to do with geographical, historical and individual identity also haunt Medem's films. Beginning with a tiny Basque valley in *Vacas* and moving on to the cosmic and global geographies of *Tierra* and *Los amantes* his films consistently represent the fragility of individual identity in a way that Joseba Gabilondo argues may have particular relevance to a history of Basque vulnerability to the vagaries of a more powerful Spanish state (*51*, p.278).

If Medem's work is linked to the outstanding success and the political complexities of so-called Basque film, it also forms a part of what Philippe Rouyer has called a kind of 'Nouvelle Vague ibérique' (*21*, p.52). Precursors can be found in a long tradition of black humour

---

[1] Medem envisaged filming *Vacas* in Euskera, but was dissuaded by Sogetel (*43*, p.195)

that dates from Goya, to Regime-director Luis Berlanga, and on to Medem's contemporary, Álex de la Iglesia. His films also have the surrealism of Luis Buñuel, the social conscience of Juan Antonio Bardem, and the metaphorical implications of Víctor Erice. International precursors in Resnais and Bergman have been noted, as well as similarities with Krzysztof Kie lowi and David Lynch (*14*, p.923; *53*). In addition, Medem cites a debt to Almodóvar, who brought Spanish film to international attention and whose films also question individual identity and gender relationships.

Film Therapy: Film and Life/ Life on Film

Rob Stone looks back at Medem's early experience on that isolated Basque hillside and suggests that:

> It is tempting to ascribe some of the sensuality and delicacy of Medem's films to this period of role reversal in which he assumed the traditional maternal duties in a country where machismo rules. Indeed the situation also suggests something of the notion of assuming another's identity that is a primary theme of his films. (*61*, p.161)

Other reviewers and critics have noted the links between his life and his film narratives. Samuel César describes *Vacas* as 'rabidly personal' (*15*, p.81) and Paul Julian Smith has called Medem a 'cineaste of subjectivity' (*59*, p.11). Medem himself describes directing as a form of therapy (*40*, p.58) and says he is unlikely to move to Hollywood as he regards film-making as a continuation of his life and might feel displaced (*1*, p.15). He describes his first three features in visceral terms: 'el orígen de *Tierra* fue el alma, mientras que *Vacas* me salió de las tripas y *La ardilla roja* de la cabeza' ('*Earth* came from my soul, *Cows* my guts and *The Red Squirrel*, my head') (9, p.37). Each is dedicated to a family member: *Vacas* to his wife Lola, *La ardilla roja*, to his daughter Alicia, *Tierra* to his son Peru, *Los amantes* to his German father, and *Lucía y el sexo* to his new partner, Montse. Alfredo Martínez Expósito notes that these dedications mark his films with a certain 'autoría y [...] propiedad'

(*53*), and Medem suggests a reason for this tendency to personalise his films in interview with Carlos Heredero (3, pp.551–586).

Video Diaries and the Collective Family Memory

His father was a keen amateur film-maker who taught Medem to use a camera, and whose videos formed an archive of family life (*3*, pp.548–551). Medem describes how his own memories gradually became overlaid with images from these films watched as a family in the darkened sitting room, to the extent that he cannot now differentiate his memories from his father's films (*44*, p.167). This ordering of the collective family memory on film is something he would return to in the motif of the family photo in *Vacas* and in *Los amantes*. Interestingly, Medem says he now has his father's films on computer, filed alongside his own, and that he hopes to edit them for his family some day (*3*, p.551). This blurring of point of view (from father to son), and the notion that film can filter into and gradually replace memory is central to Medem's work. Although he now feels ready to take on the patriarchal role as guardian of the family film archive, his teenage reaction, like Otto in *Los amantes* was to rebel. A growing awareness of the repressive, right-wing politics of the Franco Regime complicated his relationship with his father and made him focus on his mother's Basque roots. Medem implies this maternal identification provided an *alter ego* to project against his father, in a way not entirely dissimilar from Ángel's angelic *alter ego*, who provides a defence against reality in *Tierra* (*3*, pp.552–53). Rob Stone notes that 'his choice of Basqueness is a personal illustration of the fabricated myth of origins that both frees and ultimately confounds so many of his characters' (*61*, p.159). This rebellion and its links to film which is also about the 'projection' of fictional identities, dates not just from adolescence, but back to his childhood when Medem says he would take his father's camera at night 'de manera furtiva' ('on the sly') and make his own films in the family kitchen with his sister Ana (*3*, p.552).

Transpositions: the On-Screen Self

He speaks eloquently of the 'otherworldly' access his father's camera offered, and of the way it allowed him to 'entrar en lugares o atmósferas a las que no tenía acceso en los laberintos de mi cabeza y que me seducían sin que yo supiera por qué' ('to go to places, or atmospheres, in a labyrinth inside my own head that I did not normally have access to and that attracted me although I didn't know why') (*3*, p.552). Paraphrasing his comments in interview with Heredero, he says he discovered the camera could change reality, that by placing it in different locations around the house then editing what he filmed, he could change what he calls the 'space-time ratio'. He says there was a mystery in this that he could not explain, but was fascinated by because he could see that something of himself was transposed onto the film images and wanted to discover what all this might be about (*3*, p.552). This description of his first experience with a video camera, of the blending of the machine and operator, is fascinating in relation to a similar 'transposition' of 'Medem' onto his later work. In *Vacas*, Rob Stone has noted that fact and fiction blur on a claustrophobic, rural Basque hillside, and Peru's camera and Manuel's paint brush become a part of the person holding them in the same way Medem describes above. *La ardilla* debates questions raised by his father's videos: are our memories real, or do we invent them as we go along? Are they are our own, or do others impose them on us? He also explores the 'space-time ratio' in this film, parallel-cutting from present to past to illustrate the way the human mind experiences time not as a linear progression forward, but as a kind of looping process that combines memories of the past with experience in the present. *Tierra* returns obsessively to the mystery Medem discovered when he borrowed his father's camera, a mystery to do with life and its representation that Ángel studies through his futuristic optical device. Ángel is also torn between two women, as was Medem whose marriage was ending as the film premiered at Cannes, and his next film would be dedicated to his father who died a week before this premiere (*44*, p.169): the mirroring of film *diegesis* (film world), and the director's life story as told to journalists and interviewers can seem uncanny.

The 'Two' Spains: the Spanish Civil War and Franco Regime

If his early experiences with a camera suggested there was a mystery about human identity that was highlighted on film and that would haunt his later work, his racial background provided another theme. Medem describes himself as 'half French, half Basque, half German and half Valencian' (*3*, p.547), and he is particularly interested in the clash of cultures between what he sees as his more liberal, French, maternal side and the more conservative, German, paternal side. This division between liberal and conservative politics mirrors the violent divisions that that culminated in civil war in Spain from 1936–39, and the oppressive, right-wing, Franco Regime from 1936 until 1975. Almodóvar parodied the stereotyping of Spain as a country eternally divided between conservative and liberal forces in his cameo-role in *Matador* (1986) as a fashion designer staging a show called 'Divided Spain'. Medem also uses black humour to represent political and personal divisions, but his characters tend to remain traumatised by their own contradictions:

> He vivido esta contradicción desde muy joven y en mi propia casa. Me refiero por un lado la de tener un padre y una madre de ascendencias ideológicas y culturales tan distintas, con las que nos proponía aprender a convivir. Y por otro, la de saber que mi padre era un hombre sanote, campechano, encantador y muy cariñoso, era el preferido de todos los primos del lado paterno de la familia, pero que, por otra lado, estaba conforme con el régimen de Franco, aunque fuera de una manera muy simple, con muy poca ideología. Sus hermanos y primos, su familia en España, también estaban del lado de Franco. Algunos de ellos tienen tierras, inmensas fincas de caza en el sur de España. (*44*, p.170)

> I've lived this contradiction since I was very young, and in my own home. I mean, on the one hand, having parents whose ideological and cultural inheritance was so opposed, and with which we had to learn to live. And, on

> the other, knowing my father to be a good person, warm, charming and very affectionate, a favourite with all the cousins on the paternal side of the family, but knowing also, on the other hand, that he supported the Franco Regime, if only superficially, with little awareness of ideology. His siblings, cousins, and family in Spain were also on Franco's side. Some had land, huge hunting estates in the south of Spain.

Family Divisions

Given the complexities of political, regional and national, not to mention individual identity, and the way these return in his films, it is useful to consider his family background in some detail. His maternal grandfather, Albert Lafont Lafont passed French nationality to Medem's mother who spoke Basque, French and then Castilian as her third language. The same grandfather (who died when Medem was in his teens) is described by Medem as an iconic figure: cultured, sensitive, literary, passionate and romantic. His father's family, the Mendizabal, are described as more conservative, although they too had a compelling figurehead in his paternal grandmother who is described as an educated and voracious reader who, like her grandson, loved to 'buscar el lado profundo y justo de las ideas, de las personas' ('to seek out the profund and the just, both in ideas and in people') (*44*, p.169).

Medem's flair for the visual can be seen in the descriptions he provides of relatives, including his paternal grandparents, whose relationship he describes as that kind of magnetic attraction of polar opposites that recurs in his films. He describes photographs of :

> un hombre altísimo para su época, medía uno noventa y seis, y de una mujer pequeña, de expresión alegre que tocaba muy bien el piano. Siempre he pensado, viendo las pocas fotos que hay de la pareja juntos, tan opuestos en todo, que el germánico de mi abuelo tenía que

> encontrar muy sexy a la risueña hispana que era mi abuela. (*44*, p.169)

> a really tall man for those days, around one metre ninety-six, and his wife, a small, happy-looking woman, a really good pianist. I've always thought, looking at the few photographs we have of them together and noticing how completely different they were in every way, that the Germanic side of my grandfather must have found my smiling Spanish grandmother very sexy.

Medem's father, Julio, grew up and was sent to boarding school in Germany, where he joined the Hitler Youth Movement, but his mother, Medem's grandmother, returned to Spain with her seven children before the Second World War after the death of her husband (*3*, p.551). This notion of *casualidad*, a chance event that radically alters the direction of a life and, in this case, of the national identity of a family, is central to Medem's work. Similar coincidences play a vital role in the lives and deaths of his fictional characters, particularly in *Los amantes*, the film dedicated to the memory of his father.

Unrequited Love, Sports Therapy and Freud

Medem's parents moved to Madrid when his younger brother Alberto was born, the second of the five siblings, and Medem was sent to the elite *Colegio del Pilar* (*3*, p.547; *61*, p.159). At fourteen he fell in love with a girl who would go out with his brother, and the theme of painful or thwarted love recurs in his films. Medem attributes his obsessive teenage passion to the isolation he felt from the rest of a family he describes as more extrovert and less troubled (*3*, p.553; *61*, p.159). The trauma of this unmentioned and unrequited love drove him to sport. He held the national record for hurdling and might have gone on to train for the Olympics, had he not realised in time that 'el atletismo le había venido bien como terápia, pero que sus inquietudes, creía entonces, le empujaban más a estudiar la mente que a correr por los estadios' ('sport had been useful as a therapy, but his uncertainties, he thought then, were pushing him to study the mind rather than run around sports fields') (*3*, p.548). He was becoming particularly interested in Freud's work on the unconscious and took up studying medicine with a view to becoming a psychiatrist (*3*, p.553).

The Making and Mentors of 'el cineasta más inquieto y singular'

He also began to write film criticism for *La Voz de Euskadi* and moved to university in the Basque Country to finish his studies (*61*, pp.159–60). He would remain in the Basque Country for fourteen years before moving back to Madrid. While he was in San Sebastián, he made his first shorts and worked as editor and assistant director on José María Tuduri's film, *Cróncia de la segunda guerra carlista* (1987) (*3*, p.548). He then wrote the screenplay for *Vacas* that brought him the label 'el cineasta más inquieto y singular entre cuantos impulsan la renovación creativa que vive el cine español a comienzos de la década' ('the most restless and original of the directors who revolutionised Spanish film at the beginning of the 1990s') (*3*, pp.548–49).

The influence of a number of Spanish precursors has been mentioned: the iconoclast Buñuel and the famously anarchic Berlanga. Medem admired some of Juan Antonio Bardem's films and José Borau's violent 1975 rural drama, *Furtivos*, to which *Vacas* is compared (*14*, p.923). He praises Almodóvar for pushing out aesthetic and thematic boundaries to make room for the next generation of post-Franco Spanish film-makers, and considers contemporary Iván Zulueta 'un animal salvaje del cine, un verdadero artista con una capacidad para soñar muy poderosa' ('a wild beast of film, a true artist with a powerful capacity for dreams'). However, in the same interview, he expresses a particular admiration for the director Víctor Erice (*3*, p.555). Medem saw Erice's internationally renowned film, *El espíritu de la colmena* (1973), for the first time when he was seventeen, and it *was*, he says, 'un *shock* enorme'(*61*, p.160):

> Me fascinó descubrir que en la línea armónica de sus imágenes había un agujero misterioso y lúgubre, pero también dulce y cálido. Yo quería meterme ahí para crear realidades que estuvieran perforadas, mundos nacidos de la realidad, pero con un hueco por el que te puedas ir. (*3*, p.554)
>
> I was fascinated to discover that within the harmonious lines of his imagery there was also a mysterious, lugubrious hole that was, at the same time, sweet and warm. I wanted to get inside it to create realities perforated like that, worlds that were related to reality, but with a gap you could get through.

His description is highly sensitive to the ellipses (the gaps) in Erice's film narratives, but it also offers illuminating insight into his own. The description of an aesthetic 'break' that functions, like Alice's rabbit hole, as an entrance to other realities, from which we may return with our own perception of reality altered, helps to explain the enigmatic hollow tree stump that plays such a central thematic and aesthetic role in *Vacas*. Erice is clearly an important mentor:

> Su cine sigue empeñado en la búsqueda de un lenguaje propio, de unas formas que sean capaces de crear un sentido. Esa es la apuesta del cine que merece la pena, de las imágenes que te ayudan a verte a ti mismo, a sentirte libre y a ser capaz de cambiar [...]. Si hay verdad en las imágenes, es bueno que puedas sacar lo que llevas dentro y que las películas sean una prolongación de uno mismo. (*3*, p.586)
>
> His work is still about the search for a personal language, for forms capable of creating meanings. This is what makes film worth the effort, images that help you see yourself, feel free and capable of change […]. If there is truth in the images, it's good if you can pull out what is

> inside you so that your films become an extension of yourself.

Medem's films are also a 'prolongación de uno mismo' that Molina Foix suggests some detractors find narcissistic, but that has universal appeal for his supporters (*34*, p.23). Medem describes the process of making each film as a personal journey from which he never completely returns that leaves a sense of vacancy 'un agujero enorme' the next film is made to fill (*27*, p.16). His films provide what Heredero describes as a:

> discurso dialéctico de subyacente naturaleza esquizofrénico que no siempre encuentra una forma armónica de expresión, pero que se atreve a indagar – con inusitada pasión estilística de raíces poéticas – en los fantasmas más íntimos y dolorosos de su personalidad y de su vida. (*39*, p.272)

> a dialectical discourse, with underlying schizophrenic tendencies that does not always find the most harmonious form of expression, but dares to delve, with an unusual passion for style rooted in poetry, into the most intimate and painful personal fantasies that arise from on his own personality and his life.

Whether or not Medem would agree, he does think his films surpass their maker (27, p.16). Asked whether he minds if viewers think Ángel, in *Tierra*, is mad, he says that although he would rather they did not, they are entitled to their own point of view. He says, 'it's a cliché, but the film doesn't belong to me. It belongs to whoever sees it and accepts it on its own terms' (*5*, p.14). The chapters that follow take up this offer to provide a personal point of view. Personally, I tend to think Peru and Cristina die in the 'War in the Forest' despite knowing that Medem's original script followed Peru into old age. I also feel Otto dies in the plane crash despite all visual evidence to the contrary. What is significant about this is that it does not matter so much how we think the films end as what those endings convey. Medem's films reward multiple viewings and inspire multiple interpretations. This study examines the themes raised here: memory, history, war, geographic roots, the family, love, identity, the blurring of fact and fiction, the unconscious, and the evolution of the search Medem admires so much in Erice: 'la búsqueda de un lenguaje propio, de unas formas que sean capaces de crear un sentido' ('the search for a personal language, for forms capable of creating meanings').

Santaolalla says Medem's 'narratives are as full of holes as of journeys' (*57*, p. 333) and I would like to return briefly to one of the crucial journeys in Medem's life that happened before he was born. When his father came to Spain from Germany at the age of twelve, it was a chance event that removed him from association with a political ideology that would go on to become notorious for imposing a violently totalitarian point of view. It is hard not to link this chance to Medem's repeated thematic use of it in his films, to his own fierce reaction against totalitarian visions, and at times bewildering reluctance to impose a single 'point of view' on his films or on their viewers. In response to his multiple points of view and seductive circumlocutions, the following chapters examine each film as it unfolds, not because this is the most appropriate way to consider them, but because it provides a relatively straightforward path through their labyrinthine narratives. Some see Medem's grasp of narrative as less than adept (*37*, p.19), but others are more sympathetic to the poetic and haunting visual images that inspire them (*44*, p.211). Medem, as a director, is always 'más volcado sobre la visualización de las emociones que sobre la dramaturga de la narración' ('more intent on visualising emotion than dramatising plot') (*3*, p.549). The following chapters start with a synopsis and brief introduction then examine the films in close detail. They appropriate Medem's term 'secuencia cero' to discuss the opening minutes then move on to look at the films in sections (*44*, p.223). The chapters on *Vacas* and *Los amantes* are divided according to Medem's own on-screen headings, but the section headings for *La ardilla* and *Tierra* are my own, as are all translations. The discussion that follows is intended to combine description with close analysis so as to elucidate without deconstructing altogether, the elusive quality of these intricate, complex and mobile visual poems (*37*, p.19; *44*, p.23).

1. *Vacas: 'cine de mirada'*

'La metáfora de este viejo odio vasco es la rivalidad entre dos familias' (*44*, p.197)
('The rivalry between the two families is a metaphor for ancient Basque hatred')

Synopsis

Vacas is set in a small Basque valley and follows two feuding families from the Third Carlist War (1872–76) to the Spanish Civil War (1936–39). The Mendiluze[2] live on the hill, the Irigibel in the valley and their two houses are separated by a wood. The story is divided into four chapters with on-screen headings. In the first: 'The Cowardly Woodcutter (1875)', Manuel Irigibel fakes his own death in the Carlist trenches with the blood of his neighbour Carmelo

[2] I have referred to Jesús Angulo and José Luis Rebordinos for the spellings of characters' names (*44*).

Mendiluze. He deserts the battlefield, observed by mess-boy Ilegorri, hidden among a cartload of dead bodies. His ignominious escape is observed by a white cow. The second chapter, 'The Axes', begins thirty years later in spring 1905. Manuel, now an old man, paints cows obsessively and makes traps to catch the wild boar that no longer live in the wood next to his home. His dead neighbour's son, Juan, lives on the hill with his mother, Paulina, and sister, Catalina. Manuel lives in the house in the valley with his son Ignacio, Ignacio's wife Madalem, and their three daughters. Ignacio beats Juan in a wood chopping competition, then beats the local champion and wins a Dutch Friesian cow, la Pupille. Ignacio has an affair with Catalina that results in an illegitimate son, Peru. In chapter three 'The Burning Hole (Spring 1915)', Ignacio is a woodcutter of some renown, returning with his latest prize (a white car) and followed by reporters. His ten year-old son Peru steals a camera from one of the reporters and hides it in the wood where he, his half-sister Cristina and Manuel sacrifice small animals to a mysterious hollow tree stump that Manuel credits with supernatural powers. La Pupille has a fatal illness, so Manuel poisons her with mushrooms and chops off one of her hooves to 'ease' her death. Catalina disappears and Peru runs into the wood to hide from his violent uncle, who catches him and holds him upside down over the hollow tree stump now daubed with la Pupille's blood. Ilegorri takes Peru to join Ignacio and Catalina who have decided to leave for the United States and the concluding eleven years of this chapter are conveyed in letters exchanged between Cristina and Peru. In the final chapter, 'War in the Forest (Summer 1936)', the Civil War has begun, Manuel has died and Peru is a photo-journalist, sent to cover the war for an American newspaper. He and Cristina are caught up in fighting. Lucas, Ilegorri's son, offers to protect them but is shot and killed. Nationalists round up the defeated Republicans including Peru, but he appears to be saved from the firing squad by his uncle, Juan. Peru returns to the wood to find Cristina and, in the enigmatic concluding sequence, the half-siblings agree they have just seen their dead grandfather, Manuel. They then take a horse, belonging to the Nationalist soldier Lucas shot and ride off in the direction of France.

The focus zooms back onto and into the hollow tree stump as the screen fades to black.

Analysis

> El ojo de la vaca tiene un valor simbólico, pero también tiene algo de broma'
> ('The cow's eye has symbolic, but also a certain comic value') (44, p.199)

Financial restraints cut *Vacas*, the original script ended with Peru, played by Txema Blasco and by now a famous photographer living in Brasilia, preparing an exhibition of his photographs of cows (*14*, p.922). Deprived of this ending, and leaving to one side the invisible wild boar, the straw figures, the mysterious hollow tree stump, and the apparently immortal white cow, the above synopsis suggests an elaborate narrative structure. And yet *Vacas* has been described by one of its most complimentary reviewers as 'lacking in storyline' (*15*, p.81). This comment draws attention to the way the storyline, co-scripted with Michel Gaztambide, is obscured by dense visual and verbal repetitions. These create the impression not so much of a narrative unfolding as of some profoundly complex narrative event that, as Anne White notes, led early reviews to conjure the notion of 'a film which has something to say despite the fact that nobody can work out quite what it is' (*63*, p.3). This predominance of visual over chronological narrative also owes much to the influence of Basque painter, Vicente Ameztoy, who inspired the film's location, paintings and straw figures (*44*, p.192).[3]

The difficulty reviewers had deciding what the film was about also arises from the theme of lying that is a recurrent motif in Medem's work (*44*, p.53; *61*, p.161; *14*, p.922). Lying is a motif for his characters' ambivalent relationship with reality: Manuel's 'lie' sets in motion the events of *Vacas*, as Jota's does in *La ardilla*.

---

[3] Manuel's paintings are by Cecilia Roca with final touches by Ameztoy, who made the straw figures (*44*, p.205).

Ángel is repeatedly scolded by his angel for lying in *Tierra*, and the relationship between the lovers in *Los amantes* becomes a lie by omission as the step-siblings hide their relationship from their parents. The literary device of the chapter headings used in *Vacas* also helps blur fact and fiction by implying the story follows a linear progression then undermining this with an oneiric (dreamlike) aesthetic logic that eschews linear progression for spiralling repetitions (*58*, p.315–17). Like the intertitles of Buñuel's famous surrealist film *Un Chien andalou* (1929), Medem's titles guide but they do not give answers. Santaolalla notes the surrealist influence in the fusion of oppositions and the 'use of the eye as a threshold, or the inscription of the viewer's look in the text itself' (*58*, p.313).This is 'cine de mirada' ('film about looking') (*15*, p.81). Medem calls it a very visual film, 'casi muda' ('almost silent') (*44*, p.215) and its dialogue raises more questions than it provides answers. The debate as to whether the cow, la pupille, is black and white, or white and black sums this up neatly. The answer depends, of course, entirely on your point of view and serves only to highlight Medem's 'obsessive concern with the act of looking, and more particularly, a focus on the pleasures of seeing the world from different, occasionally baffling, viewpoints' (*63*, p.1).

'Secuencia cero'

Vacas is about lying, the blurring of fact and fantasy and the fundamental importance of point of view. Medem calls the opening credit sequences of his films a kind of 'secuencia cero' that is intended to seduce and hypnotise the viewer (*44*, p.223), and in *Vacas* he achieves this with an enigmatic vision of a man chopping wood. He wears a black beret, white shirt, and dark trousers and the axe lands terrifyingly close to his bare feet. Trees are in the background, and bird song can be heard over the rhythmic chopping. Focus darts from one point of view to the next as non-diegetic music harmonises with the chopping sound to construct a sinister chorus line that will recur in *La ardilla roja*. Echoes such as these in Alberto Iglesias' musical scores provide discrete reminders of the thematic repetitions that ensure Medem's reputation as an *auteur*. A chip of wood flies up in the air and the frame freezes fades to black as the title appears in red followed by the words: 'Chapter One: The Cowardly Woodcutter'.

This prelude forms a silent statement about the way the film will reframe the traditional iconography of Basque film and, in particular, its romantic idealisation of Basque masculinity and the Basque landscape (*46*, p.145; *41*, p.50; *54*, p.192; *58*, p.311). It also introduces the viewer to Medem's enigmatic and aesthetically charged formal logic. Jerky editing frames the woodcutter from different angles without actually clarifying what we are watching and it also fuses theme with form by matching each cut to the chopping action of the axe (*61*, p.162). This highly metonymical opening also condenses the themes of the film into the single action of a man chopping wood: the chopping suggests the will to dominate nature, and the terrifying proximity of feet and blade suggest vulnerability. The theme of vulnerable feet recurs when Manuel and Cristina put up the straw-figure with the scythe, and in the episode of la Pupille's fatal illness. The iconic image of the Basque woodcutter also recurs, ironically parodied in the other straw figure with the axe that never manages to catch its prey. The repetitive background chopping will also reverberate through the soundtrack until the final chapter where the sound of a banging shutter will presage Juan's return with the Nationalist firing squad. In addition to these visual and aural motifs, the flying wood chip also has symbolic repercussions. A similar chip will land in Catalina's apron. This is the kind of over-loaded visual image Medem uses for light relief (*34*, p.23): the woodchip predicts her affair with the adulterous Ignacio and Peru will be the resulting 'chip off the old block' (*41*, p.50). This 'secuencia cero' also contains self-reflexive reference to film-making that is typical of Medem. The highly artificial freeze frame and chapter heading remind us we are watching a film, not a 'true story'. They may also imply we should be careful not to let our own point of view become trapped by the screen like the wood chip in the freeze-frame. Finally, the red letters and black background connote the theme of the bloodline and the bloodshed which acts as a catalyst for this story of feuding rivals.

'El aizcolari cobarde' ('The Cowardly Woodcutter')

Focus cuts now to the Carlist trenches where the head of a dead cow dominates the foreground. Cows are fundamental to this film whose Spanish title, *Vacas*, is separated by only one consonant from the word for Basque people ('vascas') (*54*, p.192): Txargorri is the long-horned, brown farm cow, her name a reference to the red calf-genie, Txalgorri, of Basque legend. La Pupille, with the French name that suggests the pupil of an eye (*61*, p.181), is a Dutch Friesian, an expensive outsider and a threat to the native species. Then there is the mythical white cow with black points and buzzing flies that reappears as a witness, or guide to events in this 'cuento mágico sobre la endogamia de la sociedad vasca y sobre algunas de sus más antiguas mitologías' ('fairytale about an endogamous Basque society and some of its ancient myths') (*39*, p.250). Cows are central to Medem's *diegesis*, or film world: Txargorri symbolises the necessities of rural survival, la Pupille the wealth of the champion woodcutter and the white cow provides a supernatural link between life and death.

The words 'The Carlist Front, Biscay, 1875' tell us the story begins during one of a series of battles that represent 'the point of origin of Basque nationalist identity' (*54*, p.195). The same actors will play characters from different generations in the film, as if to show that civil war breeds emotional paralysis in not just one but subsequent generations of the same family. The dehumanising effect of war (*64*, p.166) is also illustrated in the way red-headed mess boy Ilegorri locates Manuel in the trenches between soldiers 200 and 230. War reduces individuals to numbers, and it reduces Manuel from a champion to a 'cowardly' woodcutter: 'an oxymoron that subverts the traditionally mythic status of the archetype' (*61*, p.162; see also *48*, p.232). Manuel Irigibel's shaking hands throw into relief Carmelo Mendiluze who is the personification of the macho hero, who celebrates the birth of his son and mocks the wife he calls a 'witch', undeterred by potential attack from the 'liberales'. A bullet ricochets off Ilegorri's metal bucket, knocking it against the terrified, clenched fist of Manuel, who instinctively punches it high up into air. This odd sequence echoes the flying wood chip of the opening freeze-frame as if Carmelo's celebration of his contribution to the patriarchal line (Juan) is, metaphorically 'punched away' by Manuel (father of Ignacio) in a sinister visual premonition of the jealous and competitive relationship their two sons will have.

Manuel freezes, but Carmelo puts his arms around him and tells him (three times) to shoot before the enemy shoot him. Ironically, it is Carmelo who is hit by an enemy bullet when Manuel finally pulls the trigger, and Manuel throws himself back, screaming, into the trench as if he too has been hit. His cowardly act of self-preservation and loss of status is symbolised in an abandoned axe that appears in the foreground. Close-ups show gruesome detail as Manuel daubs his own face with the blood pulsing from an artery in Carmelo's neck while Carmelo watches in horror repeating, three times, 'I'm not dead'. Repetitions like these give Medem's dialogues the otherworldly quality of fairytales in which threefold repetitions also traditionally have symbolic weight. A long shot shows the 'liberales' stripping Carlist bodies and loading them onto carts. Manuel stifles a cry of pain as his leg is run over, and his cowardice is witnessed by Ilegorri. The narrative cuts abruptly to the wood in which the rest of the story will be confined. This geographical enclosure will become symbolic of the emotional incarceration of Manuel having deserted the army. Manuel raises his head from the naked legs of corpses in another graphic image, not this time of his faked death, but of perverse re-birth, and as he drops to the ground from the cart his face is still covered with Carmelo's blood. A cowbell sounds and he looks downwards in submission then upwards at the cow, so that his eyes, vast and haunted like a carnavalesque mask (*58*, p.320), meet the reflecting gaze of the white cow who functions, metaphorically, as the mid-wife to his rebirth, and who will reappear throughout the film as a mysterious guide and witness to events over the next sixty-one years.

The camera zooms in on the flies buzzing around the cow's eye in one of the most striking visual images in the vivid iconography of this film. An iris shot closes and opens slowly onto a long shot of a white house and the title 'Thirty Years Later, Guipuzkoa, Spring 1905'. This temporal gap shot through the white cow's eye contracts linear time into a cyclical time. Last seen looking into a cow's eye, Manuel is now putting the finishing touches to Txargorri's eye in one of the paintings that are 'his way of taking control' (*18*, p.55). His granddaughters want to know if they are in the painting and Manuel says they are because 'everyone knows a cow won't stand still on its own, especially not in a painting', but he is lying, and as her sisters run to admire their invisible portraits, Cristina poses in Txargorri's place. She is not disturbed by her eccentric grandfather. She knew he was only painting Txargorri and her confident pose suggests she is aware of an unspoken alliance between herself and the cow.[4] The girls' mother, Madalem, scolds them for letting the cow wander off into the woods where she could eat poisonous mushrooms, go mad, and die, so Cristina runs off in the first of a series of quasi-pagan chases through the wood that punctuate the film narrative. Manuel shouts after her to watch out for wild boar as the camera pans over the wood, zooming briefly onto the buzzing, hollow tree stump then coming to rest on Txargorri and Cristina in the foreground exchanging what appear to be ironic glances, as girl and cow frame Ignacio, who is chopping wood in imitation of the woodcutter of the opening sequence.

The prelude and first chapter open and close with an image of the woodcutter that is ironically encoded and the narrative in between them has established the themes of lying, the cows, the paintings, the wood, family relationships, death, war, and patriarchy. Medem had worked on a film about the Carlist Wars (*3*, p.570) and would have known they originated in a disruption to the Spanish royal patriarchal line according to which a king's daughter usurped the throne from his brother, Carlos. This led to an uprising by Carlist supporters and decades of civil war that preceded the Basque separatist movement, and the development of its armed wing, ETA. This theme of dangerous nostalgia for patriarchal succession is hinted at in the way

[4] This unspoken alliance between a young woman and an animal recurs in Medem's next film where there is a similarly 'metaverbal' and ironic alliance between the invisible red squirrel, the same actress (Ane Sánchez) playing another incarnation of Cristina, and a young woman Sofía, who is played by Cristina's older incarnation in *Vacas*, Emma Suárez.

Carmelo's celebration of the birth of his son is juxtaposed with his horrified impotence as he dies watching Manuel daub Mendiluze blood (symbolic of the patriarchal line) over his own skin. Manuel's 'trespass' onto the symbolic bloodline of the Mendiluzes will have repercussions that are played out in each subsequent chapter. In chapter two, his son Ignacio will also symbolically 'steal' the Mendiluze bloodline by having an adulterous affair with Catalina that will produce the illegitimate son in chapter three, who will fall in love with his own half-sister in chapter four. The increasingly incestuous development of the 'bloodline' provides another metaphor for the endogamous (intermarrying), inward-looking rural valley, that may be a metaphor for the Basque Country (*44*, p.203). This opening chapter also highlights the theme of lying and the way that the horror of war and his unmentionable desertion have turned Manuel from a wood-cutting champion into a Shakespearian fool whose gnomic utterances 'question and expose the perverse hegemonic order' (*58*, p.321). The fact that Madalem is afraid of the wood and of its poisonous mushrooms that can induce madness also introduces Manuel's mildly deranged relationship with the wood. The wood comes to symbolise not only Manuel's insanity but also sexual desire (*61*, p.158), and it will be the location for the Manuel's eccentric point of view and the 'myth-related episodes' that punctuate the film (*58*, p.317).

'Las hachas' ('The Axes')

This chapter opens with Cristina and Txargorri's ironic exchange of looks as they watch Ignacio, who races off into the wood after something viewers cannot see. A similar pursuit occurs in *Tierra* when Ángel chases through a cornfield after an invisible hare and is almost shot by Patricio who mistakes him for a wild boar. Here, the pursuit is also linked to the wild boar as the implied point of view of the invisible prey is low to the ground, but the panting is human and it is Catalina who jumps up and brushes herself off at the edge of the wood. This provides a link between women and the wild boar, the wood and dangerous pursuits that will be developed.[5]

Ilegorri rides between the *caseríos* to arrange the wood-cutting competition and reveals the literal as well as the ominous figurative distance between the two *caseríos*, and the conflicts brewing within them. Catalina and Juan's discussion about the fact that Juan is the stronger but Ignacio the quicker has disturbing sexual connotations, while Ilegorri's offer to provide half the seven hundred *reales* needed to secure the wager because Ignacio 'has the blood of a champion' is met with manic laughter from Ignacio who has little faith left in the patriarchal bloodline. Editing sets up a series of enigmatic correspondences: the number 700 with which Manuel brands Txargorri's painted flank; the wooden splint on his leg that is the brand of his own unmentionable cowardice, and the shot reverse dissolves that show Ignacio and Catalina exchanging looks.

The ritual symmetry of the wood-chopping competition is visualised in the long shot of the rows of logs, and the *mise-en-scène* recalls the Carlist trenches as the same child actor (now playing Ilegorri's son Lucas) runs to and fro among the spectators. Juan wears white socks, black shoes and a black shirt, Ignacio has a black beret, white shirt and bare feet. The women stand nearby, Manuel sits apart as always, and the other spectators are relegated to the horizon as if to emphasise that this competition is a battle between the two families. A chip of wood flies into the air and Madalem watches it land in Catalina's lap, catches the smile Catalina sends Ignacio then sees Cristina smile at Catalina. These complicit exchanges echo the shots of Cristina and Txargorri that opened this chapter, as the three females (Catalina, Cristina and the cow) bond in a relationship from which Madalem is estranged. Ignacio is pronounced 'Irigibel Segundo' by the Judge, who also refers to the 'champion' Irigibel bloodline, but the mention of blood frightens Manuel for whom it is now linked not with family honour but with war, terror and guilt. He asks Cristina what the destruction of the logs is for and when she reminds him Ignacio has won the seven hundred *reales*, but he is not

---

[5] Xon de Ros points out that 'the low pans which hardly rise from the ground also draw attention to the notion of homeland' (*48*, p.226).

consoled: 'Lo tenía apuntado' ('I had it noted') he says, as if by putting the number on his painted cow's flank he had fixed the outcome. Manuel has retreated from the institutionalised horrors of the war that this competition symbolises, into an intuitive 'inner exile' of his own creation that is expressed in his paintings and in the superstitious, pagan rituals we see more of in chapter three (*44*, p.47).

The rest of this chapter consolidates Ignacio's status as a champion and overlays this simple storyline with ever more densely symbolic cinematography. Cristina and Manuel set up the spinning straw figure near the house (see *44*, p.192; *48*, p.228), Ignacio and Ilegorri return with his latest prizes (the grey horse and la Pupille) and Catalina watches from a haystack on the hill. Cinematography sets up a line of ominous correspondence. This sequence is framed by travelling shots. The first moves across a hay stack to the flanks of a cow with buzzing flies, continues up and along the cow's forelegs and stomach, then down its hind legs to the ground. The cow breaks wind and defecates as the focus tracks on through rich, bright green grass that looks fertile, but that is also sinisterly shadowed, then up the handle of the scythe to Cristina and Manuel who are securing the spinning figure, described as 'el disfraz más simbólico con el que se viste la muerte' ('the most symbolic disguise for death in this film') (*64*, p.167). Manuel warns that the scythe is so sharp it could cut off their feet. As Ignacio arrives with Ilegorri, a long shot picks out Catalina on a haystack, lifting her skirts and stamping. Ilegorri suggests another competition with Juan and a long-distance zoom implies Ignacio and Catalina share a glance that ruffles her hair. This over-loaded zoom reframes her ironically, as a witch or pagan goddess of fertility holding an enormous (phallic) piece of wood, that de Ros links to the 'atmosphere of witchcraft in another Basque filmmaker Pedro Olea's film *Akelarre* (1983)' (*48*, p.233). Catalina tells Juan that Ignacio will not compete with him again, as if that briefly shared gaze informed her Ignacio would not fight because he has already won everything he wanted: the title of champion and Juan's sister.

Their silent exchange sets off the next chain of events. As Manuel looks into la Pupille's eye to see if she is in calf, an iris shot closes and opens onto the house on the hill where Paulina predicts that if Catalina continues looking at that 'son of a coward' she will bring a curse on the whole family. Juan is furious that Ignacio will not compete again and he hurls his axe deep into the wood like the Basa-Juan of Basque mythology. Medem says this image of a woodsman hurling an axe into a wood was the visual inspiration for the entire script, and if the Carlist Wars symbolise the origins of Basque nationalism, this symbolises the legendary birth of the Basque race (*44*, p.192). According to folklore, the Basque Country was originally cultivated by a race called the Basa-Juan. The first Basque male tricked them and stole the seed that allowed the Basque Country to be colonised by humans. Infuriated, the Basa-Juan hurled an axe after the man, splitting in two the tree behind which he was hiding. Traditionally the Basa-Juan was represented as a giant, a benign wood spirit, or an ogre with a witch for a wife, and in Medem's film, Juan, this reincarnation of the Basa-Juan, lives with a mother referred to as a witch.

Cristina runs to the woods, to see if Juan's axe has hit Ignacio. She falls to the ground as an axe lands threateningly close to her in a way that White links back to the chip of wood that landed in Catalina's apron in the second chapter (*63*, p. 14). This enigmatic sequence links Catalina with the wild boar again, and Ignacio with the mysterious straw man Manuel has set up to catch the non-existent wild boar (*39*, p. 254). Catalina's question, 'What have you cut from me?' makes explicit the link between the axe and sex that is conveyed in another travelling shot that closes this chapter and opens the next. The camera tracks over her blue socks, legs, white shirt, and beyond the couple through the undergrowth to the bark of a tree and the mysterious hollow stump on which appear the words 'Chapter Three: The Burning Hole'. The heightened artificiality of the cinematography marks the transition to a chapter that will focus on this symbolic hollow tree stump as well as the repercussions of this adulterous encounter.

'El agujero encendido' ('The Burning Hole')

La Pupille is giving birth to her calf. Ignacio has his arm inside her and the three girls are pulling on the rope attached to the unborn calf's legs, Madalem is holding the cow's head, and Manuel cheers them on. This is clearly a family affair the irony of which is underscored when the focus cuts, as the calf is born, to Catalina and Peru walking out of the wood and the title 'Ten Years Later: Spring, 1915'. Peru's existence is explicitly linked to the birth of la Pupille's calf in an unflattering reflection of the value of women in rural communities. Juan has become jealously possessive of his sister and his illegitimate nephew, but Peru rebels against his uncle, and spends his time with Manuel and Cristina (now played by Emma Suárez). María Pilar Rodríguez notes that Peru represents a 'line of flight'. He rejects his uncle's authority and the wood-cutting tradition, and disrupts the patriarchal line from Irigibel 1 to Irigibel II (*55*, p.82), to align himself with Manuel's world of pagan superstition, imaginary boar and flesh sacrifices. This is a world in which women have the upper hand. Peru throws his sacrificial mouse in clumsily, but Cristina hits the target, the middle of hollow stump, first time. Their confusing rituals with the 'agujero encendido' derive not from patriarchal Catholicism, but from ancient, chthonic (related to the earth) Basque religions whose supernatural spirits live on or under the ground and who prefer underground sacrifices.

Providing a link with ancient Basque legend, the tree is also, as de Ros notes, a reminder of the famous Basque town of Guernica:

> A symbolic repository of Basque identity, Guernica's millenarian oak tree, the traditional site for the elders' assembly, represents the nation's struggle for self-determination. An allusion to Guernica is found in the title superimposed in the opening sequence of Medem's film: *Frente Carlista, Bizkaia, 1875*. We are situated in the third Carlist War which historians refer to as 'la Guerra contra el centralism'. It was precisely in 1875 when the Carlist king Carlos VII took the oath in Guernica to uphold the *fueros*. In *Vacas* there is a

> mysterious oak stump endowed with strange powers standing in the wood which the two farmhouses share. Already the presence of communal woodland is a reminder of the prerogatives sanctioned by the *fueros*. Later […] we learn that when the tree is fed with flesh its roots give off an eerie glow. It is not difficult to see in this image a metaphorical embodiment of Basque national consciousness, with a history marked by the blood of numerous victims, whether of terrorism or repression, whose deaths have often been used to rekindle the flames of nationalism. (*48*, p.229)

Ignacio has won another competition and among his prizes is a new car. On-going family tension is revealed in the way Madalem flinches as he kisses her for the photographers, who ask him to pose with his axe in the air. Madalem and Peru exchange glances. Manuel peers through the lens of the reporter's camera. Manuel is transfixed by the camera and the potential of this entirely new, mechanical point of view that he will ask Peru to steal for the three of them.

At night the focus moves to the bedroom Catalina shares with her son. Peru watches her run into the wood to meet Ignacio. Catalina tells Ignacio Juan is going mad and suggests they run away to America (Ignacio has told her there is a war in Europe, so France is not a good idea). The mythical white cow appears on the road in front of them and Catalina is shown returning to her room to find Juan asleep next to Peru. Juan attacks her, shouting 'I don't want to kill you. I'm your brother' in a scene that has disturbingly incestuous connotations, and that Anne White links with the way Yerma strangles her husband, Juan, in Lorca's play of the same name. She notes that although Juan does not kill his sister his attack is 'an intriguing inversion of Lorca's scenario, with a male, Juan, now cast in the role of an individual unhinged by a desperate yearning to produce offspring' and that this 'effectively also puts an end to his chances of either becoming a surrogate parent to her son, Peru, or of fathering a child of his own to continue the Mendiluze line' (*63*, p.6). Peru screams, thumping the bed convulsively with his head. When

Juan leaves, he and Catalina exchange, almost word for word, the dialogue about running away she had moments earlier with Ignacio, although this time Juan takes Catalina's part and Catalina takes Ignacio's. White also notes this repetition and that Catalina's statement that she wants to escape is repeated in Cristina's letter to Peru and again in the closing dialogue between the two half-siblings (*63*, p.13). This echoing repetition of dialogue, like the use of the same actors to play different parts, accentuates their representation as ciphers rather than individuals, suggesting that any attempt to lead an autonomous life will always by compromised by their shared destiny.

Cutting from this disturbing sequence to daylight, Manuel poses the family for a portrait taken with his stolen camera. An iris shot of the family cuts to Peru's eye, linking earlier iris shots of Manuel's eye with the boy who 'inherits his grandfather's attraction for those artificial "eyes" which can mediate and open up reality' (*58*, p.321).[6] Surreal editing follows: iris shots of the moon, insects, wildlife, and Peru's head behind a camera looking uncannily like a cow's. Peru asks what is on the other side of the hollow tree stump, and Manuel claims, paradoxically, that Peru and Cristina are on the other side, and that he is the only one on this side but that he will soon be joined by la Pupille who is dying. Cristina looks through the oblong viewfinder as if to demonstrate what it is like to look 'from the other side'. The focus cuts to the spinning scythe-figure and dreamlike framing of the three relatives as if they were a formal cinematic still-life on the theme of observation: Cristina watches the scythe-figure, Peru watches her, Manuel paints la Pupille, while the figure with the scythe and the red beret spins in ominous circles. Peru and Cristina run off into the wood to find mushrooms for Pupille, accompanied by non-diegetic operatic accompaniment, travelling shots, and close-ups of sinister-looking red berries. Extreme close-

[6] De Ros links this sequence to the film's revision of cinematic Basque iconography, noting that Manuel's photo shoot is reminiscent of the 'brothers Mauro and Víctor Azkona, well-known professional photographers, who wrote, photographed and directed in 1928 a rural drama entitled *El mayorazgo de Baxterrechea* which is now treasured by the Filmoteca Vasca' (*48*, p.233).

ups of the mushrooms and Peru's questions about breasts suggest, once more, that sex and insanity are dangerously linked in this wood.

Manuel chops off la Pupille's hoof he says, to 'ease' her death. Peru wakes to find his mother has gone and thinks Juan has killed her. Madalem discovers the mutilated cow and attacks Manuel, kicking him and screaming that he is a coward who should have died in the war. Cristina tells her Manuel is mad, as if the truth might break the cycle of violence, and her grandfather sinks his bloody axe into one of the wooden pillars. The reverberations of this are conveyed in a travelling shot along the wooden beams that cuts to Peru asking after his missing mother, then to Cristina holding the scythe-wielding figure while Manuel places pieces of the dead cow's meat in a circle around it. Peru runs into the wood shouting that his uncle has murdered his mother, but Juan appears abruptly behind him. Like Ignacio, Juan is now linked to the straw axe-man, his sudden appearance is jerky and automated as if he were controlled, like Manuel's straw-man, by some external force. He holds Peru headfirst over the log, sadistically claiming the blood belongs to his dead mother who is down there waiting for him, but he is lying. Cristina explains the blood is la Pupille's as if there were nothing odd in the fact that she and Manuel have thrown the infected flesh of a dead cow into a hollow tree stump. In Medem's films, it is the women who calm and deflate the more hysterical emotional reactions of the men, but Peru has reason to be hysterical: his face is still covered with the blood Juan told him was his mother's when Ilegorri arrives on horseback to take him to his mother who is leaving for North America with Ignacio. Like Manuel, Peru has undergone a vicious symbolic rebirth but, unlike his grandfather, it is a prelude to his departure, not his return to the valley.

At this point cinematography frames the half-siblings as if they were lovers being pulled apart (*61*, p.165), and the chapter concludes with a montage of dream-like episodes that mark time with letters exchanged in narrative voice-over. Peru's are read by Manuel (blending and blurring the different generations again) and they include photographs of Peru's new house and his car. The wood is represented in strangely cartoon-esque shots of wild animals: a lizard, a bird, a mouse, the hollow stump, rain, a cow bell, as if to suggest Cristina is trapped in an enchanted place, her blue headscarf a reminder of simple, fairytale illustrations. The letters summarise the passing of time in fragments: Peru marries a redhead, who is now pregnant. Cristina tells him that is a coincidence because she too was involved with a red-head, Lucas, but they have separated. Cristina sees wild boar two days walk from the wood and the chapter closes with an enigmatic close-up of her face in profile through blurred leaves. Her final letter says Manuel is painting wounded cows and wants to die. There is a dissolve to the hollow stump, point of view tracking from the (invisible) boar, and the straw axe-man hits the ground, as if confirming Manuel's death wish. Dissolves and disorientating zooms scan the trees as she says war has broken out and she wants to leave. After being shot in a highly artificial and enigmatically still profile, she turns and walks off left as the red words of the final chapter appear.

'Guerra en el bosque' ('War in the Woods')

Cristina walks down a leafy path towards the camera and title frame, and the focus cuts to a shot of her scything grass with Madalem, as a loose shutter bangs in the abandoned house on the hill. Point-of-view tracking through the ferns mimics Ignacio's pursuit of Catalina at the beginning of chapter two, another blurring of generations as Peru now tracks Cristina. The oddly truncated zoom that frames their meeting appears to abstract them from time and place. Manuel is dead, and Cristina shows Peru the wooden canvases he has left whose three-panel construction suggests a pagan triptych, a tribute to the godlike omniscience of his cows. The paintings are enigmatic recreations of symbolic events in the film: la Pupille bleeding as if she has been shot; Peru and Cristina sitting on a two-headed cow, and a painting called 'War' that refers to the Carlist trenches. In Manuel's recreation, the child Ilegorri has horns like a cow, or a Viking warrior, and Manuel and Carmelo's heads have been replaced with cows' or bulls' heads. Faced with these poignant, violent images, Peru only comments that whenever he wants to think of someone he thinks of Cristina and she agrees that she does too. It is as if they, like

Manuel, can no longer respond to life, but only to an intertwined destiny represented in Manuel's painting by the two-headed cow. At night, Peru trespasses in Cristina's room and sees the photo of his and her father, Ignacio with an axe over his shoulder, and the photograph of his own pregnant wife. He is then shown looking towards the wood from the hay loft as his echoing voice-off calls to Cristina. Editing cuts from Cristina and Lucas having sex watched by the white cow, to Manuel's painting, 'War' linking the notion of sex with rivalry and death once more. The surreal lack of continuity in these shots suggests they may be an atavistic projection of Peru's that recalls the assignations between his mother and Ignacio that sealed the destiny of these two half-siblings.

The following day, boys are using the red-bereted-scythe-wielding figure for target practice. The red-beret now represents the enemy, Carlist collusion with right-wing nationalists (*48*, p.232). Nationalist troops are said to be on their way and Madalem orders the men into the wood. She has usurped the patriarchal role in the small community left in the valley. The enemy are invisible at first like Manuel's wild boar, but their red berets begin to appear among the trees recalling the shots of the red berries in chapter three and linking the notion of the enemy to some poisonous natural growth. As the battle begins, the focus cuts to the grass-stained forelegs of the white cow walking down a path, then back to Peru's camera, bottom of frame, as Lucas shoots a Nationalist from his horse. Composition frames the threesome oddly: Cristina sits in the foreground looking up at Peru, whose head is in line with the top of the frame. He is kneeling, his up-stretched arms holding his own camera out of frame, as he leans against Lucas's legs that are moving convulsively with every shot he takes. Fern stalks in the foreground suggest prison bars. The focus cuts to a horse, then to the white cow that turns and walks off, as if followed by the horse, then back to Peru pushing Cristina to the ground. This gesture echoes the past, Ignacio pushed Catalina to the ground in the same way in chapter two. Gun fire links sexual passion and death as Lucas body falls next to the couple. Cristina screams and runs. Chased by Peru, she falls into a catatonic state and a terrified Nationalist soldier discovers Peru (the soldier's terror is another echo from the past, of the terrified Manuel in the trenches). Nationalist soldiers shoot black-bereted prisoners, dragging off their bodies, and providing more narrative loops backwards to the Carlist trenches as the film approaches its denouement. The officer in charge mocks Peru who is pretending to be American. Peru is substituting his family bloodline in a way that parallels Manuel: Lucas's dead body is dragged past and observed by Peru, echoing the dragging of Carmelo's dead body observed by Ilegorri in chapter one.

Peru is lined up to face the firing squad next to Ilegorri, but Juan says he is the son of Carlist soldiers and should not be killed. Ilegorri confirms this, but Juan shoots him in the stomach, bringing to a brutal end the filmic 'lines' that have traced the fate of this red-headed family: Ilegorri ran along the line of the trenches, his son, Lucas ran along the line of spectators and now, sixty years on, Ilegorri is shot in a line-up by Juan. Peru falls back with the dead Republicans, in another echo of Manuel in the trenches, but he appears to jump back, unhurt, and runs to find Cristina. The sound of a cowbell and a close-up of the straw axe-man bowing to the ground precede a shot of Cristina high up next to a tree asking what has happened. The couple exchange dream-like statements. Peru says the soldiers took his camera and that he is nothing without it, but Cristina shows him he still has it in his hand. She says she fell asleep and saw Manuel. Peru claims to have seen him too. The horse neighs and Cristina, echoing Catalina's conversation with Ignacio in chapter three, asks if there is a war in France. They get on the horse, unmoved by the body of Nationalist soldier whose foot Peru unceremoniously dislodges from the stirrup. Peru says he will sacrifice his life for Cristina and she says 'good', but she is not responding to him, this is one of the deflating responses common to Medem's women. She is hungry and has found food in the saddlebag (*58*, pp.321–2). The focus cuts back to the white cow and their voices are heard off. Cristina tells Peru to hold her closer and whisper in her ear; Peru says he loves her more than anything in the world as the focus shifts from the white cow to the hollow tree stump. The voices-off continue: Cristina says 'Yo te he estado esperando para quererte toda la vida' ('I've been waiting to love you all my life'), and Peru says he will never let her go. Cristina repeats Manuel's line 'Esto es importante' ('that is important') and Peru concurs, also quoting Manuel, 'Muy importante' ('very important'), as the screen fades to black. Cristina's last statement is 'We're getting there'. Medem explains that Cristina's declaration of love, not in the original script, was for his wife, Lola, to whom the film is dedicated, and that 'diciendo eso entramos por el agujero del bosque que se lleva a los dos amantes de allí' ('with these words we enter the hole in the wood that takes the lovers away'). In this instance, the hollow stump is, as Medem describes it a visual metaphor for the paradox that eternal love does not always last a lifetime (*44*, p.205).

Conclusion

For Medem, *Vacas* was a film about conscience and consciousness (*44*, p.197) that uses the natural landscape as a metaphor for some kind of collective unconscious (*44*, p.203). Manuel's 'cowardice' is a fear of war and of death, but it is also a rejection of the cyclical history of war. As a result, time is represented as something rational and linear that can be conjured up in dates and causal chronologies, but is also represented as emotional and cyclical. Medem says the rural location allowed him the freedom to present the story in what he describes as the 'metarrealidad' of the natural world (*3*, p.560), and Yates notes the 'thinness of fairy tale in character and in motivation' (*18*, p.55). The narrative repetitions suggest the two families become increasingly trapped between this half-unconscious, 'meta-real' fairytale world and some kind of empirical, patriarchal order. The shots through the cow's eye that Manuel and Peru imitate when they look through the stolen camera may move, but the characters remain trapped in the frame, and the narrative theme of entrapment is clearly expressed in the formal and aesthetic structure of the cinematography, in the use of the zoom and the iris shots. Ilegorri may save Peru from his vicious uncle like a knight in a fairy tale and Peru may move to the States, but he cannot escape the destiny that frames all Medem's characters' actions like the lens that pulls them back to a hollow stump, or to the eye of an omniscient cow (*58*, p.322). Vidal notes that the 'círculo se cierra en el bosque encantado' ('circle closes in the enchanted forest' *17*, p.8), while White notes that in 'the film's closing scene the voices of the dead lovers, Peru and Cristina, are heard in conjunction with a shot of the black void of the *agujero encendido*, turning womb into tomb' (*63*, p.13).

The film makes repeated reference to framing: Manuel's wooden canvases, Peru's camera and the mythical white cow's eye represent confinement to an inevitable cycle that is represented in the repeated natural motifs: the fern grove; the pagan chase through the wood; the letting and distribution of blood; the hollow tree stump; the cows, and the invisible boars. In addition to this dangerous and cyclical natural world, 'framing' symbolises another dangerous cycle that is to do with the human world and the imposition of a single political, emotional, or even filmic 'point of view'. The focus on point of view in Medem's work has its origins in early twentieth-century surrealism (*58*, p.313). His narratives, like those of the surrealists, highlight the fact that a world that appears ordered, rational and empirical, may be disrupted at any moment by the unconscious and irrational.

Jesús Angulo and José Luis Rebordinos suggest that Manuel's retreat into insanity is a form of protest against war that the other characters express in their desire to leave. They then link this to Medem's description of leaving the Basque Country for Madrid as a kind of liberation (*44*, p. 58). De Ros links the implied flight at the end of *Vacas* to a comment made by Juanma Bajo Ulloa that successful Basque directors 'son precisamente quienes han huido del País Vasco' ('are precisely those who have fled from the Basque Country') (*48*, p.233). Medem has pointed out that the script was based on the notion of an invisible rival, symbolised by the wild boar Manuel fails to catch with his straw axe-man. The rival is a projection, 'la paranoia de crearte un fantasma' ('a paranoid fantasy') (*3*, p.569). It is the externalisation of an inner conflict and as the rival is a part of the self any attempt to conquer it will be self-defeating, setting in motion cycle of violence that will not be resolved. Comparisons with ETA and the armed struggle for Basque independence have been made. Cerdán notes that the valley functions as a synecdoche of the Basque Country and that the ambiguous end pulls the spectator back into the hollow 'epicentro tanto de la locura de los personajes como del infierno del territorio' ('the epicentre, not only of the characters' insanity, but also of a territorial hell') (*14*, p.923). Medem has said that 'el peor fascismo es el interno [...]. Por eso en la película no se ve nunca al enemigo, éste casi no existe, porque lo que me interesaba era la tensión entre los propios vascos' ('The worst fascism is internal [...] That is why, in the film, you never see the enemy, it's almost as if it doesn't exist, because what interested me more was the tension between the Basques themselves' (*3*, p.570).

The motif of the hollow tree stump anticipates *Tierra*'s island 'aún atravesada por agujeros de misterio' ('still pierced by mysterious holes'). It symbolises the door to another world to which Manuel has escaped (*44*, p.55) in a film in which 'one-dimensional or essentialist notions of identity and subjectivity are ruthlessly exposed' (*58*, p.312). Medem acknowledges his debt to Vicente Ameztoy, who was himself an inspiration for Manuel (*44*, p.205), and whose exhibition, *Karne y Clorofila* was an inspiration for the otherworldly rural landscape. Ameztoy's half-joking, half-fascinated representation was of a 'naturaleza frondosa en la que crece el sexo entre la muerte, rodeada de moscas, esos paisajes con la líbido en flor, llenos de figures humanas de paja' ('a leafy natural world where sex grows next to death, surrounded by flies, landscapes with a flowering libido, full of straw figures'). Medem recognised in it a world that could form part of the new world of '"el aizkolari cobarde" que se exilia de este mundo cuando su conciencia atraviesa el ojo de una vaca' ('the "cowardly woodcutter" who exiles himself from this world when his conscience passes through the eye of a cow') (*44*, p.192). For Medem, 'el ojo de la vaca refleja esa mirada irónica en la que se condensa la historia' ('the cow's eye reflects the ironic gaze through which the story is condensed') (*15*, p.82). Cows eyes also represent Manuel's guilt and the way that 'en su subconsciente, se da cuenta de que ver no es suficiente, hay que *mirar* ('he subconsciously realises that seeing is not enough, you have to look') (*15*, p.82). The cow's eye-view is also a metaphor for Becks' perception of the way Medem 'radically restructures the visual regime of "looking" and offers a critique of the male-centered "gaze" prevalent in Western filmmaking' (*46*, p.159). The recurring visual metaphors to do with looking ('cine de mirada') highlight the dangers of a totalitarian gaze, whether it is imposed by an aesthetic recreation (such as Manuel's paintings), by reportage (Peru's photographs), or by the firing squad, and the dangers are repeatedly highlighted in cinematography that refracts point of view and underlines human pretension by subjecting the film's action to the ironic and impassive gaze of the white cow.

2. *La ardilla roja:* Mad Boy's Love Song?

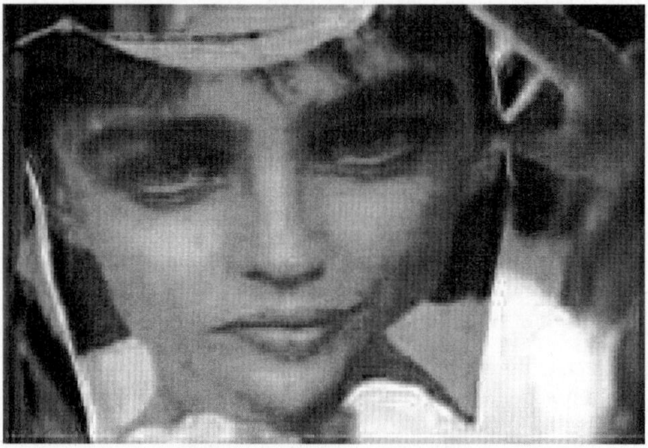

I dreamed that you bewitched me into bed
And sung me moon-struck, kissed me quite insane.
(I think I made you up inside my head.)

('Mad Girl's Love Song', Sylvia Plath)

Synopsis

Jota is the former lead singer in a band called 'The Flies'. His girlfriend and former band member, Eli, has left him, taking the car. He is considering suicide by jumping onto the rocks in the sea below his flat in San Sebastián, when an unknown woman crashes her motorcycle through the railings further up and lands on the beach below. Running to help, he discovers she has no idea who she is, and sees this as an opportunity to substitute her for his ex-girlfriend, convincing the ambulance men and doctors at the hospital that she is his girlfriend 'Lisa'. 'Lisa' appears to go along with his story, and the couple leave, on her bike, to go camping at a site called '*The Red*

Squirrel' near a reservoir in La Rioja. They meet a family from Vitoria and 'Lisa' becomes friendly with the downtrodden wife, Carmen, who is bullied by her 'machista' taxi-driver husband, Antón. The son Carmen adores, Alberto, and his little sister Cristina play 'happy families' with Ana, the daughter of a widow, Begoña, who is happy to leave Ana with Carmen's family as she is entirely focussed on finding a substitute for her German husband, Otto, who died in a car crash. 'Lisa' faints when Alberto tries to put her under a hypnotic trance. Meanwhile Félix, Sofía's violent ex-husband, has arrived at her brother Salvador's flat. A radio announcement placed by Félix is broadcast, asking for any information about the whereabouts of a 'mentally disturbed' young woman driving a motorbike and Alberto recognises the registration number as Sofía's. Jota attempts to reassure the family, but Antón phones Félix and tells him where they are. Félix arrives at the campsite, and cuts his cheek with a pair of scissors to demonstrate how profound his love is for Sofía. Sofía escapes on her bike, but the two men follow her in Félix's car. Félix crashes into the reservoir and is killed, but Jota survives. He returns to San Sebastián, and puts out his own announcement for Sofía. Looking at an old photograph of himself and his ex-girlfriend, Eli, he is inspired, as it were by Sofía's voice, to make the connection between her and Salvador, the man he met at the hospital after her accident. Salvador tells him Sofía is working at the Madrid zoo. Jota borrows Salvador's car to go and find her in the red squirrel enclosure at the zoo. Then he lies to her again, claiming he knew all along she had not lost her memory. He tells her he has written a new song for her, and accuses her of not knowing enough about him. A red squirrel hidden in the trees defecates on his head, as if commenting on his rather hypocritical speech, and the couple hug.

Analysis

Medem began work on the script for *La ardilla* before *Vacas* but says he got stuck at the campsite and began writing *Vacas*, which then was taken up by Sogetel (*44*, p.192). *Vacas*' success set up such daunting expectations that Medem refers to it ironically as 'mi rival más duro, el más peligroso' ('my toughest, most dangerous rival',

10). Despite his fears and an initially negative response from critics in Madrid to *La ardilla* (*44*, p. 217; *61*, p.182; *60*, p.128), international praise led to speculation about an American remake and interest from Kubrick and Spielberg (*13*, p.42; *44*, p.225).

Medem admits there are elements of himself in Jota (*27*, p.16). Jota is Spanish for the letter 'J' and Medem's first name begins with J., Jota is a champion runner and Medem was a champion hurdler, and it was unrequited love that pushed the adolescent Medem into athletics. This story about obsessive passion, is reminiscent of Medem's experience when he says that for some years after falling in love with the girl who went out with his brother, her image or rather his image of her, was 'detrás de mi cabeza, mirándome, como si estuviera asomada al balcón de mi conciencia. ('behind my head, watching me, as if she were leaning over the balcony of my consciousness') (*3*, p.553). He says *La ardilla* is 'una parábola contra el machismo en clave de comedia de misterio. Una ficción fabricada desde la psicología masculina, de la que se deduce una lección moral contra la relación de propiedad que el hombre ejerce sobre la mujer' ('A parable against 'machismo' in the form of a mystery comedy. A story made up by a man, that offers a moral lesson about the way men try to exert ownership over women') (*44*, p.128). First love and institutionalised machismo both construct femininity as an enigma that has little to do with the living female. For Medem, 'la premisa principal de la película era una violación moral en toda regla, de un hombre hacia una mujer' ('the film's central premise is an absolute moral violation of a woman by a man'). But the 'game begins', as he puts it, when Sofía takes the role on in a way that 'prometía ser una interesante burla contra el machismo' ('promised to be an interesting joke on machismo'). At the same time he refers to the story as a 'metáfora del amor' ('a metaphor for love'): a metaphor for the way love stimulates reinvention, making lovers behave temporarily as more ideal versions of themselves (*44*, p.209). The theme of love envisaged as the creation of an enigma from the murky depths of the human psyche is central to the film and is symbolised, as in *Vacas*, by a strikingly metonymical opening sequence. The previous chapter on *Vacas* was divided by the chapter headings Medem inserted into the film, this chapter on *La ardilla* is also divided into sections, but the subheadings are, of course, my own.

'Secuencia cero'

The underwater scene is symbolic of the watery depths of the human psyche. In this case the symbolic lake has added resonance because it is artificial. It is, like Jota's psyche, 'man-made'. A forest has been flooded to create a reservoir, hence the apparent contradiction of trees seen underwater that also hints at the ambiguities and confusions that drive the film narrative. As it unfolds we realise these trees are rooted in land flooded to create the reservoir near 'The Red Squirrel' campsite: Sofía will win her swimming race against Alberto in it, her dangerous ex-husband, Félix, will die in it, and, metaphorically, the 'new man' Jota will be reborn from it. After the watery capitals that compose the title frame, the focus jumps abruptly back to the sea front of San Sebastián and an apparently suicidal leading man.

Sofía's Fall

Tracking downwards and zooming slowly in over the back of Jota's head and the waves crashing below, this is the first of a sequence of shots of the back of characters' heads in a film that emphasises how little they ever know about one another. Enigmatic shots of Jota and the waves as he swears and kicks the metal barrier imply he is suicidal but lacks the courage to jump. He is distracted by a motorbike crashing through the barrier further up and the tracking shot that links the reverberations along the railing from the bike to Jota's hands is a common motif in Medem's work, representing characters linked and trapped by a shared destiny. The focus then moves to handheld point of view as Jota runs towards the victim of the accident who will become the female object of desire in this strangely abortive Pygmalion narrative (*61*, p.182; *56*, p.156).

In a film so focussed on gender there are numerous ironic references to masculine flaws. Male narcissism is satirised in Jota's white T-shirt that has an inflated image of his own face on it and in his macho posturing with the motorbike. Antón, the taxi driver, personifies aggressive male competition, boasting about his driving and saying women cannot drive because they have no balls. He has passed his arrogance on to his son Alberto, who tries to compete with Jota and patronise Sofía. There is also more light-hearted representation of sexism with wider repercussions for the plot when Jota tells Alberto 'no te fíes nunca de esas rubias' ('never trust these blondes'). The supposedly amnesiac Sofía is not at all amused when she asks Jota whether she is really good at anything and he says, 'Yes, shoes', claiming she used to work in a shoe shop that closed. 'Menos mal' ('thank goodness') is her heartfelt reply. For Medem, this is a tale about the problems in any heterosexual relationship, and he puts machismo first on his list: 'El machismo, por supuesto, y también la pasión, la falsedad, los celos' ('Machismo, of course, and also passion, lies and jealousy') (*10*).

The joking asides to gender prejudice and machismo begin with Jota's assumption that the crash victim is male. Sofía is hidden by the crash helmet that frames her face for the ironic shot reverse shots (that is, shots from the point of view of one, then the other character) that provide 'alternating points of view in the battle between the sexes' (*61*, p.167). The use of the frame as a self-reflexive reference to the film screen, recurrent in *Vacas*, is less prevalent in *La ardilla* but remains an important motif. A series of 'frames' gesture self-reflexively to the borders of the film screen, and act as a warning to watch out for our point of view. There are the shots through Sofía's helmet (*61*, p.167), and the one of her used in countless publicity shots, her Mona Lisa smile framed and slightly distorted by the jukebox glass. There are fewer references to painting, so prevalent in *Vacas*, but Jota's flat contains the incongruously romantic lake scene with its lovers symbolically silhouetted from behind, and the equally symbolic abstract painting of two primitive male figures fighting. These prefigure the confusing dream sequence of the battle between Félix and Jota that provides another way of framing the main narrative, and finally, there is the photograph that will reveal the 'true' story.

Jota tells the crash victim (mixing his metaphors in a way that gestures back to the opening underwater sequence and forward to *Tierra*) that she looks like a 'fish out of water' thrown from the sky. She has no documents and no memory. Jota searches for her papers intrusively and answers her question about the colour of her eyes with a lie. He says they are 'ojos azules que se enredan' ('tangled, blue eyes'), but Sofía's eyes are brown and the phrase is a lyric he wrote for his ex-girlfriend, Elisa. He continues lying when the ambulance men arrive, claiming he jumped off the bike before it hit the railings. The ambulance man's comment that if they had crashed further down the road she would have been killed on the rocks also functions as an ironic reference to Jota's aborted suicide on the same rocks. The *double-entendres* continue in the ambulance, where Sofía says 'tengo un sueño que me muero' meaning, figuratively, 'I'm dead tired' and, literally, 'I'm dreaming I'm dying'. Her near-death encounter and this comment symbolise the fact that the person she was (Sofía) is 'dying' in order to make way for the identity (Lisa) that Jota is conjuring up for her from memories of his ex-girlfriend Elisa.

The central focus on lying continues in hospital administration. Jota is sent to Salvador's office (neither realising at this point that he is the victim's brother). As Jota enters the office, Salvador is on the phone lying to the radio presenter of the show *A vida o muerte*. He says he's alone, but Jota is in the room with him; he says he is in the dark, but the room is light; he does not deny that he is 'triste y desatendida' ('sad and alone'), the feminine ending of the second adjective colluding with the radio presenter's heterosexist assumption he is a woman. He is sending a message to Luis Alfonso, his beloved 'gasolinero', who is listening to it from Félix's car radio in a nearby garage. This location sets up cross-cutting between Jota and Félix, whom we do not see and do not know at this point in the story. Félix drives off and the inflated sound of an ominous gust of wind and the loaded symbolism of the cloth falling from the windscreen of his rapidly accelerating car are accompanied by the opening bars of Nat King Cole's 'Let There be Love'. The song opens at a crescendo, and then, cutting back to Salvador and Jota in the hospital, fades to a soft accompaniment of their dialogue about names, occupations and addresses. The lines of the song, with their disregard for names ('Let there be you, […] me'), ironically underscore the contradiction between the need for names to satisfy hospital bureaucracy, and Jota's desire to keep hold of a woman he only cares about as a representation of a possible 'you', or rather, as a substitute for his lost 'you', Elisa. The music becomes increasingly soft, then crescendos as a hit-and-run victim is brought into the hospital screaming (momentarily we associate the screaming with the woman Jota just brought in). This unknown victim acts as a warning: again, we do not know who she is, but her arrival links Cole's lyrics to Félix's murderous driving in his urgent desire to catch Sofía on her bike. The song then fades altogether as we cut to a shot of Sofía, laughing and unharmed, except for a persistent case of feigned amnesia.

Songs are fundamental to *La ardilla*. Basque singer Txetxo Bengoetxea sang the two songs Medem wrote for Jota (*44*, p.211). The line 'ojos azules que se enredan' is a metonym for way love songs, like Jota's lie, are also made up of fictionalised, idealised images of the beloved. Sofía appears to resist this at first. She disagrees with the name he gives her: 'Yo no me llamo Lisa' ('I'm not called Lisa') and says she knows her eyes are not blue. She will challenge him throughout the film, sometimes appearing to collude in her own subordination to his fantasy, sometimes deliberately thwarting his attempts to control her. Their ambivalent power relationship is framed ominously here when Jota leans over her and extends the quote into what could be read as a pejorative reference to female speech: 'ojos azules que se enredan y una larga lengua de gata' ('tangled blue eyes and a long cat's tongue'). He kisses her possessively. A doctor explains the words are lyrics, but Jota's proprietorial attitude is disturbing.

The fissures in their power relationship are illustrated in the subsequent dream sequence back at Jota's flat that is overlaid with commentary from a TV documentary about endangered, devious red squirrels who have to make up 'plots behind men's backs'. Jota dreams of Eli, his ex-girlfriend and Sofía. A close-up of brunette Eli moves left to right out of frame and is replaced with blond Sofía. This swap represents the way Jota, like the endangered squirrel, is projecting his own 'subtle plot'. The fusion of dream and commentary links the squirrels to women, an endangered species that can 'crack nuts'. This ironic reference to emasculation continues in the comment that the 'worst thing that can happen is to lose their tail', which links the squirrels to men. The music speeds up ominously, the dream version of Sofía introduces herself as 'tu novia amnésica' ('your amnesiac girlfriend'), the alarm goes off, and Jota wakes up. The dream links the women to the devious squirrels but also to water, the close-ups of sinuous hands on Jota's body physically gesture to the way their image is slipping into his psyche. Two different women are blending in the watery element of Jota's unconscious and this symbolic link between Jota's unconscious, sinuous, devious women, and water recurs when water turns out to be a natural element for Sofía, whom he will refer to as his 'sirena' ('mermaid'), and in dialogue spoken by the violet-haired waitress who says she loves swimming in the lake at night, but warns them that the water becomes full of hands ('se llena de manos').

Jota has determined on a name for his creation, and returns to the hospital confidently claiming to be a relative of Elisa Matximbarrena, the woman in Room 112. Like the soldiers at the beginning of *Vacas*, Sofía is reduced to a number for the opening *mise-en-scène* of this story about misplaced identity. He steals 'Fuentes' for her second surname from the label on Salvador's white coat and Salvador (who is, of course, Sofía's brother) remarks on the coincidence. This is the first of many ironic references to the way lies so often turn out, in this film, to be true. Paul Julian Smith notes that 'the psychological truth of the characters is shown (to us, to them) to be founded on falsehood. Indeed, the lies improvised by Jota as the narrative progresses prove literally to be true' (*60*, p.136), and Philippe Rouyer describes the narrative as 'un monde irréel, presque cartoonesque, où il suffit d'énoncer les choses pour qu'elles se réalisent' ('an unreal, almost cartoon world in which you only have to say something for it to become true') (*21*, p.52).

Sofía wakes to her new boyfriend Jota, who tells her they have been living together for four years in a flat opposite the sea and that they had planned to leave today on a camping holiday. She asks whether she is very much in love with him and he says they are. As they kiss the focus cuts back to his flat and the real source of this fantasy love. Jota is confessing to a friend that Eli has left him and taken the car (even in this, poor Jota lags behind, the friend already knows). We then see him reject the T-shirt with Eli's face from the pile of clothes he is packing for Sofía. The focus moves around his flat, picking out the romantic pastoral scene on his wall and closing in on the anonymous couple silhouetted by a lake. At the hospital Jota is frustrated in his attempt to get Sofía out quickly by a group of people around her bed observing her reaction to photographs of the backs of various heads designed to stimulate her memory. With hindsight we see these include photographs of Félix, but for now all that is conveyed is the ominous sound of wind blowing again and Sofía's disturbed reaction. She instinctively says Félix's name twice, but gives other photographs names beginning with J. (including Medem's own, Julio) as if to confirm that Jota is the most important person in her life, but she then discovers his real name is Alberto.

The Escape

Jota takes Sofía from the hospital in Eli's clothes and on her bike (miraculously mended) that he pretends he does not know how to drive. Where the lyrics of 'Let There be Love' provided a counterpart earlier to the Félix's compulsive pursuit of Sofía and his ploughing down of pedestrians in the name of love, Jota's song 'Elisa' accompanies this journey. The song is heard on Luis Alfonso's radio as the couple drive past and continues as incidental music over their exit from San Sebastián. It also dissolves into Alberto Iglesias' musical score. Here the song is crucial to the parallel-cutting that will set Jota up as a retrogressive narcissist, as the flashbacks to the video shoot reveal the combination of narcissism, vivid imagination, and desire for the woman who has left him that motivate Jota.

Medem uses the video shoot to provide more information about Jota. He says that, since the shoot was set in the past it amused him to make it 'muy remoto, un pasado de aspecto prehistórico, con esos abrigos de piel de vaca y esa especie de danza india' ('very distant, prehistoric, with coats made of cowhide and a kind of native american dance') (*44*, p.211).[7] This parodic reference to distant origins is important to the way this sequence frames Jota. It sets him up visually, in terms of the clothes he is wearing and what he is doing, but adds little depth to his character. This, ironically, tells us as much about Jota as we need to know. The video shoot suggests that Jota's masquerade, his public performance, is based on a rather desperate form of nostalgia. He was the lead singer in a now defunct rock band 'Las moscas' ('The Flies'). Eli, the dark-haired woman in his dream, was the keyboard player, and the musical and visual clues establish Jota's shallow theatricality. The parallel montage in this sequence confirms the hypocritical ease with which he is replacing Eli. The seamless fusion of past and present women is wittily demonstrated by the lyrics that accompany the shot of the present from Jota's point of view through his helmet's metal frame: 'sueño que vivo dentro de ti, y vivo rodeado de hierro' ('I dream I live inside you, surrounded by metal'). Echoes of this song punctuate the film score, as the song and the CD cover showing the band in their 'prehistoric' costumes, come to signify Jota's lies and self-delusion. At this point, the confusion of past and present, and the fact we know so little about Jota add to the tension of this hybrid romantic comedy / thriller.

'The Red Squirrel' Campsite

The couple stop to decide which campsite to go to and Lisa asks what Jota is good at. She then tests his self-proclaimed 'reflejos prodigiosos' ('phenomenal reflexes') and the action replay provided by Jota, showing how he flung one crash helmet in the air to catch the other, emphasises the artificiality of the film medium, the role of the games and competition in its narrative, and satirises conventional TV

[7] It was choreographed by his sister Ana, who also appears on percussion. Medem makes a moving tribute to her memory in relation to this video shoot (*44*, p.211)

slo-mo repetitions of outstanding male success in sport (*61*, p.170). At the campsite, their own fake relationship is mimicked by the fake location, the vast cartoon squirrel advertises a site which is clearly a long way from its self-professed 'ambiente mediterráneo' ('Mediterranean atmosphere'). They meet the couple from Vitoria who will act as a dark foil to their own imaginary relationship. When Carmen invites them to a meal, Jota becomes nervous and begins to dictate Sofía's behaviour telling her not to get too friendly and not to tell them she has lost her memory, then joking that she doesn't like children and he doesn't like the taxi driver. His nervousness implies that he may be, as Stone suggests, 'terrified of autonomous females' (*61*, p.169).

The evening meal brings further character development. A mildly sinister cutaway to the cartoon squirrel's face is accompanied by ominous music, as Lisa drops a glass under the table to test Jota's 'prodigious reflexes' again. She seems to be enjoying the precedent he has set for making up their identities as they go along. She says Jota is a running champion. Alberto, Carmen and Antón's son, is a champion runner too. Alberto has failed his music exam, but, in an unintended insult to Jota, Carmen says she doesn't mind because music doesn't count ('la música no cuenta'). Sofía goes on to claim she is a swimming champion, and Jota says they met winning races, but his sarcastic tone suggests anxiety about the high claims she is making for their invented *personae*. These competitive introductions are interrupted by the arrival of Ana's mother Begoña, who reveals her lack of social and maternal skills by offering money for the expensive prawns her daughter does not eat. Carmen tells Sofía that Begoña was widowed two years earlier when her husband fell asleep at the wheel, and that she is looking for a German replacement 'Era alemán y ahora quiere repetir' ('He was German and now she wants another one').

This reference to another lover looking, like Jota, for a replacement, is followed by an enigmatic shot from the point of view of the invisible squirrel running down the tree to pick up a prawn Sofía has dropped, then Jota's confusion as the prawn disappears and an extreme close-up of the empty shell falling. Enigmatic shots from the squirrel's point of view punctuate the narrative, reflecting Sofía's sometimes odd behaviour and suggesting she may know more than we think (*61*, p.181). The meal ends and Sofía confides in Carmen details of a marriage she should not be able to remember while Jota eavesdrops from the tent. The Nat King Cole lyrics recur. Carmen is framed by the caravan window, whistling along as she washes up, and the song is played over a shot from her point of view of Sofía undressing that cuts to the taxi, then back to Carmen who turns up the volume to sing along. When she turns up the radio, the counterpoint already set up in the previous sequence between the gentle 'gasolinero' looking for love and a murderous male driver continues as editing cuts to Félix, shot from the back seat of his Ford Capri, also singing along. The cloth from the earlier sequence is replaced by the body of the pedestrian hitting the windscreen. There is a scream, silence, then cut to Sofía waking up in the tent, an extreme close-up of the hairs lifting on her arms, the sound of her frightened breathing, then a cut to the lake shore. This sequence of cross-cutting overlaid with the sounds of 'Let There be Love' is framed with brief shots of the water rising and falling on the shores of the lake, as if to suggest something monstrous rising from the deep. Editing suggests Sofiá has a kind of sixth sense warning her of Félix's violence and she is terrified. For Medem this is the only aspect of the game Sofía does not control: 'El único aspecto que Lisa parece no saber dominar es su propio miedo, que se exterioriza cuando se le eriza la pelusa de la piel' ('The only aspect Lisa seems not to control is her own fear, shown in the lifting of the hairs on her skin') (*44*, p.131).

The following day Sofía trumps the German's operatic singing in the shower with the aria, 'Kommt ein schlanker Bursch gegangen' from Weber's *Der Freischütz* (a song in which a woman boasts of her successful seduction of men). She takes up Alberto's challenge to a swimming race and beats him. In the evening, Begoña's German lover puts on 'Let There Be Love' and sings along to the woman he is about to abandon. This cynical representation of love has parallels with Jota and Sofía's conversation. The song plays now over parallel-cutting to Félix and Jota. Jota and Sofía are lying to each other about a sex life they have not shared. Sofía claims she likes 'pinning Jota down with her legs so he can't escape', but flashbacks suggest she is addressing these comments to an unseen companion on a plane (Félix). Parallel-cutting from the present ('Let There Be Love') to the past ('Elisa') links the three main characters, and heightens the tension. This evening ends in enigmatic hints: staggering back to the tent, Sofía shouts out 'Salvador' to the radio programme *A vida o muerte*, then laughs and falls over. The sex scene that follows includes shots of Félix's hands and a tracking shot from the point of view of the squirrel as a large pine cone falls and dents Antón's white taxi.

Jota is becoming frustrated with his rebellious creation, his version of Elisa Doolittle in Shaw's *Pygmalion*. Annoyed that she seems to be telling him things he doesn't know, he moans: 'Aquí todo es mentira. Eli, ¿tú sabes en que mundo vivimos?' ('Everything's a lie here. Eli, do you know what world we live in?'). But Sofía picks him up on the slip with the name, and his petulant self-defence suggests he has more problems with knowing what world they live in than Sofía. Later, Alberto 'hypnotises' Cristina. She plays along, winking conspiratorially at Sofía, as if to say that female submission is just a charade, but it is best the men do not find out. Further evidence of their collusion with the natural world against the 'man-made' world is provided when Cristina can see the elusive squirrel. Antón is attempting to knock his bonnet back into shape after it was hit by the pinecone presumably thrown by the invisible squirrel.

The battle between Sofía and Jota intensifies. She defies his demand that she have nothing more to do with the family, and invites Carmen to stay in 'their' flat by the seaside. Sofía is now wearing the T-shirt with Jota's face on it, and the role-reversal continues when they swim in the reservoir and the line 'pareces un pez fuera del agua' ('you look like a fish out of water') is now spoken by Sofía in a similar kind of repetition and substitution of dialogue to the one used in *Vacas* to undermine the characters' autonomy. A long shot of the two of them on the hill echoes the silhouette of the couple in the painting in Jota's flat. Jota is becoming suspicious. He accuses Sofía, hypocritically, of playing games with him. The confusion mounts when Alberto appears to hypnotise Sofía and she faints. The children are sent away while Jota interrogates her and her replies are cross-cut with scenes of Félix arriving at Salvador's flat and throwing a book onto the floor that falls open at a photo of a red squirrel. Luis Alfonso, who is there, links Félix to the man in the red Ford Capri and Salvador is clearly worried about Sofía. When she comes round she claims to remember nothing and Jota appears satisfied. But, for the viewer, Félix's claim that he needs her as much as his own 'liver, bones, lungs' is as disturbing as his claim that Sofía is disturbed and needs him because he is her angel.

After Sofía's fainting episode Jota says complacently that he prefers her amnesiac, but Sofía is fighting back. She symbolically castrates Alberto in a way Medem describes as the weak punishing and ridiculing the strong (*44*, p.213), and the competitive Alberto's humiliation is conveyed in a cutaway to a motorcyclist crashing in the middle of a race. But the next 'family' meal is interrupted by the radio announcement and it is Alberto, who recognises the registration of Sofía's bike. Jota launches into an inspired lie that is, as always in this narrative, implausibly close to the truth, but while he is in full flow a pinecone lands on his head and he faints at sight of his own blood. This is a form of come-uppance dealt by the metaphorical and invisible squirrel for his possessive fictionalising of Sofía.

Jota's Fall

Jota is now flat on his back in a direct echo and reversal of the opening sequence that extends to the dialogue when Sofía questions him about the colour of his eyes. They're blue, Jota replies, so Sofía knows he is fine. She goes to the jukebox and puts on 'Elisa', smiling enigmatically in collusion with the jukebox which frames her face. Ostensibly, she is helping to bring him around, but her ironic expression suggests she also intends to bring him around from his own self-delusion. She knows who he is and the song, like the invisible squirrel that may have dropped a pine cone on his head, acts as a warning to him about inventing lives. Like the endangered squirrels of the documentary, she adapts rapidly to the challenges of a changing environment, whereas Jota is clinging to the past. The song, 'Elisa', represents his addiction to nostalgia. The video is dated, as are the band's posturing, their costume and the lyrics about the 'mystery' of woman. Jota's tenacious grip on his own fantasy world is about to be shaken. He feels increasingly threatened in his self-ordained role as Sofía's protector and his aggressive stance at the phone is not, as he claims, to protect Antón and his family, but a response to a growing awareness of his own fragile façade.

When Antón attempts to phone the number given in the radio announcement, Sofía thanks him, ironically, for being so brave, but Carmen scolds him for interfering and editing cuts from Sofía and Jota in the tent, to a moon and cloud shot reminiscent of Buñuel, to the lake and shallow waters, a shot of the sun through the tent and the underwater trees of the opening shots that are now explained as Sofía's point of view, swimming underwater. This surreal editing and the underwater shot introduce the dream sequence that follows, the water symbolising entry into Sofía's unconscious. It is set in a mock 'wild west' location where men fight over woman. This is Sofía's dream, so it is made up of fragments of dialogue, the recollection perhaps of being slapped by Alberto, and imagery that clarifies her fear of and residual attraction to Félix, as well as her sense that Jota is no physical match for her psychotic ex-husband. The dream sequence ends with Jota beaten into submission, asking Sofía to tell Félix where she is, but Félix claims to know already and says that Jota has no idea whom he is dealing with because Sofía 'tiene una mente portentosa' ('has a portentous mind').

Daylight again and the radio broadcast for Sofía is repeated. Cristina can now recite all the words to it, and her game of 'happy families' with Alberto and Ana continues to infuriate Antón. Alberto wants to know why Jota calls Sofía Lisa and Jota, his lies encroaching ever closer to the truth, claims it is a reference to his favourite song, 'Elisa'. He then agrees with Alberto that he fainted at the sight of his own blood, and the focus moves to Cristina and Carmen in the caravan, cleaning. Cristina tells her mother she loves her, and Carmen says she is too good and will suffer greatly. Antonio Sánchez highlights the way this exchange functions as a metonym for the wider narrative theme of male violence and control, noting that it is a poignant reminder of the way 'patriarchal values and attitudes

[…] remain fossilized in the collective unconscious' and of 'the long psychological internalization of male violence' (*56*, p.159). From this, Carmen's veiled warning to her daughter about the treachery of men, the focus cuts to Jota at the bar phoning Félix.

Jota warns Félix off, but someone else, presumably the intrusive Antón, has already phoned him from Vitoria. A sequence of rapid cutting follows, the cartoon squirrel, a night scene on a motorway, a car driving fast, Sofía sleeping, then to the following morning and an unexplained close-up of a wooden crate. Sofía is hanging up her swimming costume, Begoña is weeping over Otto, and Carmen is worried about Antón and Alberto who are three hours late. Antón draws up in cloud of dust, and Sofía slaps him for upsetting Carmen. He tells Jota if he cannot control his girlfriend he, Antón, will, and Sánchez notes the interesting shift of allegiances as the family defend Sofía (*56*, p.158). In the middle of the confusion Carmen says to Sofía: 'Hay alguien en tu ropa' ('There's someone in your clothes'). Félix has appeared at her washing line, but the words are also a reference to the metaphorical, dreamlike images of hands insinuating themselves into clothes that have punctuated the narrative.

The mood of the sequence that follows is dictated by the psychotic Félix and has similar qualities to the other dream sequences, including word for word repetition of dialogue from Sofía's dream. As Stone notes, 'Medem emphasises this eruption of the subconscious with a furious mix of strange angles, distorting lenses and low-level shots that suggest fear and retribution on a mythic scale' (*61*, p.172). It is the youngest male Alberto, (Jota's ironical namesake) who challenges Félix, answering back on Jota's behalf. The dreamlike *mise-en-scène* continues as Félix repeats the speech heard earlier in Sofía's dream in which he calls Jota 'un lagarto vanidoso, un enano mentiroso, más pequeño que un violador' ('a vain lizard, a lying dwarf, lower than a rapist') and claims that she and he are fused 'nuestras mentes siguen fundidos', that she has been lying to Jota who cannot hope to understand her, that he is her angel and that without her he, Félix, does not exist. Alberto challenges him again, going against type to say they should ask Sofía who she wants to be with. He also contradicts Félix when he says that without Sofía his blood stops flowing, but Félix takes a pair of scissors from the wooden crate shown earlier and cuts off a piece of his own cheek to prove it. His role as a more violent *doppelgänger* for the self-deluded and lying Jota is clear as he lies: '¿No veis? Me corto y no sangro' ('Can't you see? I've cut myself and I'm not bleeding'). Alberto, echoing Jota earlier, faints at the blood. Sofía runs to her bike and drives off.

The Escape

Jota's champion running skills are now displayed in the surreal chase sequence where he catches up with and jumps into Félix's car. The men fight and their physical similarity is highlighted. Félix's manic laughter in response to Jota's comment about his driving is a *non sequitur*. It is also an echo of Ignacio's manic laugh in *Vacas* in reaction to suggestion of his father's prowess as a wood cutter. He asks if Jota is resigned to his fate as he drives off the edge of the road into the reservoir. Both men scream in what looks like a comic homage to *Thelma and Louise* (1991). The car lands in the water and sinks to the bottom of lake. There is a shot of bubbles, then Jota still in his white T-shirt trapped by the safety belt he fastened earlier when commenting about Félix's driving. Félix is dead. Cut to trees, fade to black.

Epilogue

The concluding sequences open with Jota's voice off. It is a ghostly echo calling: 'Elisa ven he visto la muerte desde muy cerca, me dolían los dientes, olía a tierra al fondo del pantano'('Elisa, come, I've seen death close to, my teeth hurt, it smelt of earth at bottom of the reservoir'). In the last of the many parallels and role-reversals, Jota, like Salvador, is broadcasting a plea for Sofía to contact him via the radio show, which is heard by Salvador at the hospital, Luis Alfonso at the garage, and Carmen, crying, and presumably back in domestic servitude in Vitoria. Still calling her Lisa, he dedicates to her, not the new song he says he has written for her, but the old song

'Elisa'. The song induces a moment of Proustian illumination, via the photograph of himself with Eli. He goes to the hospital to find out she knew all along that he was 'making her up'. As the representative 'new man' in this story, he still does not have his own transport and has to ask to borrow Salvador's car to go and find her at the Madrid Zoo where she is now working.

Jota drives sensibly, unlike Félix, he finds a sign for the squirrel enclosure, an echo of the cartoon squirrel identifying the campsite, and the camera tracks to a wire door through which Jota puts his hand, pushing his way through leaves in an echo of the undergrowth of the wood in *Vacas*. Sofía is wearing red overalls, identifying her, as have her other red clothes, with the endangered squirrel. She is crouching in a clearing with her back to him. Still lying to her, and with his customary and unself-conscious hypocrisy, he claims to have known all along she was lying to him, and, in unconscious repetition of Félix's comment to him about Sofía he says she still doesn't know what he has inside ('Aún no sabes lo que llevo dentro'), at which point a squirrel defecates on his head, and he says 'mierda' ('shit'), which, as Sánchez notes, is an ironic deflation of his pretensions to inner depth (*56*, p.158). He says that at least he has written a song, while she has just wasted her time, and credits roll to the lyrics of the love song he has written for his 'novia amnésica' ('amnesiac lover'). Sofía retains her enigmatic 'Mona Lisa' smile, and her attraction to Jota remains unclear. The final love song is calmer than 'Elisa' and its lyrics recycle the conversation they had about sex heard earlier in the film. Félix's masochistic impulse to live through her is echoed in the line 'te doy toda mi voz' ('I give you all my voice'), but the urge to control her is tempered by the words 'así te siento, así te vivo, así te doy mi amor' ('This is the way I feel you, I live you, I give you my love') that suggest a more mature acknowledgement that love is only ever offered to an image of the person as she or he is 'lived', or 'felt' by the lover. The fact that he reclaims Sofía as 'mi novia amnésica' ('my amnesiac lover'), might still be read as ironic coda to the film, confirming the relative irrelevance of the real identity of the beloved.

Conclusion

La ardilla roja has less obvious links with the Basque country than *Vacas* and its central concern is heterosexual relationships. Nonetheless critics have read the regional question in the way the film sends up of notions of geographic 'origins' with its artificial lake and its 'Mediterranean' campsite located in La Rioja. La Rioja is, as Smith notes, nowhere near the Mediterranean, it is between the Basque country and Castile. Jordan and Morgan-Tamosunas note the 'cerebral, complex [...] parodic, postmodern send-up of personal as well as cultural "origins"' (*41*, p.101) and Stone suggests a link via Sofía, to the 'post-Franco rise of feminism' that may have parallels 'with the struggle for autonomy of regions such as the Basque Country (*61*, p.169). Smith also wonders whether the 'ironically named Félix' ('happy') (*60*, p.135) could be seen as a 'displacement of the historically and politically specific violence of ETA which Medem does not care to represent directly' (*60*, p.140).

The mixed critical response the film received may be linked to its paradoxical representation of love as a form of violently aggressive or possessive projection onto women. Heredero criticises the fact that a film presented as anti-'machista' falls into the trap of becoming 'machista' itself in its representation of woman as a mystery (*39*, p. 257). Linking this to patriarchal Judeo-Christian and folkloric depictions of dangerous women and witches, he is concerned that Sofía appears to collude in it all too lightly (*39*, p.258). He also thinks the narrative gets stuck ('se estanca') at the camp site and begins to go around in circles ('empieza a dar vueltas sobre sí misma') (*39*, p.260). This is interesting, as Medem also says he got blocked at the campsite and left this script to write *Vacas*. Heredero's conclusions are damning. He says the film's 'estética heteroclíta' ('strange style') reminds him of *Blue Velvet* (David Lynch, 1986) and of Almodóvar at his most banal, and he particularly laments the dreadful band (*39*, p.260). He concludes that Medem's visual inventiveness is badly let down by the script (*39*, p.260–61).

Medem was concerned that critics such as Heredero found *La ardilla* 'machista' (*44*, p.209). He says the character of Sofía is 'escondida entre lo aparente y lo oculto' ('hidden between what you can see and what you can't') (*44*, p.130), and his defence of the woman/squirrel metaphor is that it is an allusion to the way women are forced to behave 'para librarse de una situación machista' ('to free themselves from a male-dominated situation') (*44*, p.211). Perhaps the problem with the depiction of Sofía should be approached from another angle. Medem's response to the question whether he feels more comfortable working with female or male actors is cryptic. He says that 'en general mis películas se enamoran más de ellas que de ellos. Me refiero a ese ojo que los mira, a esa pasión inevitable que la pantalla también quiere contar' ('in general my films fall in love more with the women than the men. I mean the eye that watches them, the inevitable passion that the screen also wants to convey') (*44*, p. 215). Medem's vision of a supposedly neutral film screen is problematic, but then he freely admits that he, 'como hombre, siempre me pongo en la postura de ellos. Pero también trato de comprenderlas a ellas' ('as a man, I am always speaking from their position, but I try to understand women as well') (10). Although he is, as all of us are, restricted to his own point of view, *La ardilla*'s humorous representation of male weakness and vanity raises important questions about gender prejudice and it is perhaps too much to expect the film to answer them as well. Smith comments on its 'reproduction of feminine stereotypes in a radically weakened form' (*60*, p.136) and, as Sánchez concludes, it certainly 'provides a further departure from Medem's earlier representation of women in *Vacas* by highlighting and challenging the representation of them as the objects of men's desire' (*56*, p.160). Finally, to return to the Plath poem used as an epigraph for this chapter, the precedent for making up the objects of our desire is not necessarily set by men:

> I shut my eyes and all the world drops dead;
> I lift my lids and all is born again.
> (I think I made you up inside my head.)

3. *Tierra:* 'Le silence éternel de ces espaces infinis m'effraie.'[8]

'The eternal silence of infinite space terrifies me'

'Es importante el café, sobre todo para mi cabeza'
'Coffee's important, especially for my head'

Synopsis

Ángel is sent by his uncle's firm to a small rural community to exterminate a plague of woodlice that is making the regional wine taste 'earthy'. Confused and recently an inmate in a psychiatric ward, he describes himself as 'half-angel, half-man' and appears to be followed around by an angelic *alter-ego* played by the same actor, who is invisible to the other characters in the film. Arriving to carry out his job, he brakes to avoid hitting a sheep in the middle of the road and carries it on his shoulders to a gypsy caravan where he

8 'Pensée', no.301, in H.F. Stewart, *Pascal's Apology for Religion* (Cambridge: Cambridge University Press, 1948), p.103.

meets Manuel, the leader of the gypsy community. He tells Manuel that this is the first time he has visited this area but that he feels a sense of *déjà vu*. He says he is looking for about twenty men to work for him for two months, then the split between the real and the surreal widens as Charly, Manuel's fourteen year-old son, throws a stone at a wooden post. Ángel follows its trajectory to discover a dead sheepdog and a shepherd surrounded by four dead sheep, all burnt by a lightning bolt. The shepherd begins to breathe again when Ángel arrives and they have a conversation about death during which the shepherd claims Mari, a nineteen year old who lives nearby with her brother Alberto, threw the thunderbolt that killed him. Ángel explains that this means Ulloa was plugged for a moment into the clouds and the shepherd confirms that he feels a hole from the top of his head right through his body. Ángel offers the dead sheep to the gypsies but they reject them because they are, Ángel claims, superstitious. Ulloa dies again and Ángel closes his eyes.

Enigmatic connections between this world and the next are suggested throughout the film. Ángel meets thirty-year-old Ángela who lives with her father Tomás, husband Patricio and daughter, also called Ángela. Ángela and Tomás taste the wine with Ángel. Ángel says the effect the woodlice have on the taste of the wine is a mystery, nobody understands why it occurs. All agree that they like the taste anyway and Ángel wonders why anyone should want to exterminate the woodlice. Tomás explains that he and his wife (who was pregnant with Ángela at the time) killed a plague of them thirty years earlier with boiling water, sulphur, and lime. He is still grieving for his wife who died a year earlier so Ángel offers him one of the dead sheep to cheer him up. Ángel begins to tell them how he found the dead sheep on the road, but his angel reminds him he is lying and he corrects himself. Ángela notices the sheep has blue flecks in its eyes and studies Ángel's eyes carefully. Ángel meets Ángela's daughter and husband Patricio who proudly shows him his tractor. Patricio is having an affair with Mari and Ángel is drawn into conflict with him, because he is attracted to both women. The rivalry between the two men increases until Patricio is killed by a thunderbolt. Ángel exterminates the plague of woodlice, offends the gypsies by accusing them falsely of stealing, then offends the women by not being able to choose between them. When he realises his mistake and comes to apologise to the gypsies Charly throws a stone at him. At the film's conclusion, he wakes up in hospital and chooses to leave with Mari. His angelic *alter ego* remains behind with Ángela.

Analysis

The links between Medem's films are suggested not only in the use of the same actors but also in repeated fragments of dialogue and storylines. Carlos Heredero reminds us that Jota said the reservoir in which Félix died smelt of earth and that he claimed to be Sofía's 'angel' (*39*, p.261). In *Tierra* the actor who played Félix plays a man who has apparently returned to earth as an angel. Heredero also notes the similar depiction of women as the product of male fantasy and that Kara Elejalde, who played taxi-driver in *La ardilla*, plays a similarly misogynist character in this film (*39*, pp.261–62). Rob Stone suggests that the highly artificial and surreal filming of Sofía's crash at the beginning of *La ardilla* shows her falling straight down from the sky like an astronaut (*61*, p.167) and *Tierra* concerns another 'fallen angel', a man who believes he has been sent from the heavens and whose job requires protective clothing that makes him look like an astronaut.

The character of Sofía in *La ardilla* was inspired by legends that also influence the dominant feminine incarnation in *Tierra* (*44*, p.130). The script developed from one Medem had begun about eight years earlier based on the seductive folklorical 'dama de Amboto', whom Medem describes as 'una adolescente muy sexual' (*2*, p.66; see also *44*, p.221; *5*, *37*). She is related to the Basque goddess Amari, who was said to live underground and whose worshippers left offerings for her in caves. The iconic image of seductive teenager, Mari, is also filmed 'underground' in a bar, *La letxe basterretxe*, which has walls made out of earth (*2*, p.66). [9] Mari, like her

---

[9] The title of Alberto's bar is a reference to another script Medem did not film, called *La leche Basterretxe*, which, like *Vacas* contained the image of

legendary counterparts, seduces Ángel with a writhing dance that may, as Paul Julian Smith dryly notes, have helped the film's 'unlikely box-office success in the domestic market' (*59*, p.22–23).

In addition to its source in the seductive women of Basque legend, the story is inspired by the seventeenth century French philosopher Pascal, whose philosophical reflections on human existence and religious faith were published after his death in the form of numbered 'thoughts', *Pensées*. The published script of *Tierra* (*65*) has as an epigraph part of Pascal's 'pensée' no. 148: 'Ce n'est point de l'espace que je dois chercher ma dignité, mais c'est du règlement de ma pensée. Par l'espace, l'univers me comprend et m'engloutit comme un point; par la pensée, je le comprends.'[10] Viewed from the perspective of space, Pascal suggests, a human being is just a tiny dot ('point') swallowed up by the vast cosmos, so that human dignity cannot not found in our physical relationship to space but in the control of the human mind that is flexible enough to be able to comprehend the cosmos. This epigraph illustrates the problem that torments Ángel (*44*, p.221). The contradiction between the vast parameters of the human mind and the insignificance of the human body in relation to space is one Ángel struggles with. As Pascal suggests and the evocative opening sequence of *Tierra* illustrates, Ángel is tormented by the fact that he is just a tiny 'point' in relation to the cosmos, smaller even than the woodlice he views from the godlike perspective of his 'geoscopio'. In order to live without anxiety he needs to bring under control his thoughts that spiral outwards to encompass multiple worlds, so as to focus on the eponymous earth on which he lives.

Medem says this film contains more of himself than his earlier films (*1*, p.15). His own marriage was coming to an end as it premiered at Cannes, and filming had been held up for some time by

---

the woodcutter flinging an axe after a hidden rival and also included a sequence in which film fans discussed the famous Basque film, *El mayorazgo de Basterretxe* 1928 by brothers Víctor and Mauro Azkona (*44*, p.191; *39*, p. 253).

[10] H.F. Stewart, *Pascal's Apology for Religion* (Cambridge: Cambridge Univesirty Press, 1948), p.49.

Antonio Banderas for whom the role of Ángel was intended, inspired by the character he played in Almodóvar's *Átame* (1990) (*44*, p.227). Banderas finally rejected the role in favour of Trueba's film *Too Much* (1996) and Medem suggests the actor was torn like Ángel, pulled in the direction of north America by his own version of Mari (*44*, pp. 227–29).[11] While waiting for Banderas, Medem wrote the script for Mari's diaries that he envisaged filming in black and white at the same time as *Tierra*, so viewers would have the benefit of her point of view as well as Ángel's. He describes the stories of Ángel and Mari as 'los costados de una historia común situada entre las estrellas y la cochinilla, entre la imaginación y la realidad' ('both sides of a shared story that takes place between the stars and the woodlice, between imagination and reality') (*65*, p.14). However, it was not filmed and was used only as a reference for the young actress, Silke, for whom, according to Medem 'fue muy duro, le parecía espantoso el personaje' ('it was hard because she was shocked by her character') (*6; 44*, p.231). Carmelo Gómez, originally contracted to play Patricio, took over the lead, and his role went to Karra Elejalde (*44*, p.231). Medem worked with Spain's foremost cinematographer Javier Aguirresarobe for this film, and praises him for 'images [...] endowed with a kind of subjective charge', as well as for his contribution towards making it 'clear that Ángel's world is absurd as well as tragic' (*5*, p.14).

As Isabel Santaolalla notes, 'Medem's films prioritize the look as the instrument guaranteeing access to those multiple layers of reality, connecting those worlds which are located "at a slight angle" to reality' (*57*, p.334). In none of his films, perhaps, is this so pronounced as in *Tierra*. Its visual parameters range, as the extraordinary opening *mise-en-scène* makes clear, from long shots of an apparently infinite cosmos to extreme close-ups of the woodlice. This visual scale illustrates the unbridgeable distance between human beings and the cosmos that highlights the theme of existential angst and the fear of death. Medem says 'Ángel necesita proyectar parte de su esencia en un ser que no existe, que ya ha muerto, para sentirse

---

[11] Antonio Banderas left his wife, Spanish actress Ana Leza, for American actress, Melanie Phillips.

menos vulnerable a la muerte y quitar importancia al hecho de morir' ('Angel needs to project part of himself onto a being who does not exist, who has already died, to feel less vulnerable to death and to take away the importance of dying') (*65*, p.13). Its verbal parameters also transcend the normal filmic range in the form of Mari's diary and the essay 'El complejo de Ángel' ('Angel's Complex') that were published with the film script. In his essay Medem clarifies that:

> Ángel es un ser que vive dentro de sí mismo, perdido en el cosmos sonoro de su imaginación, bajo la bóveda celeste de su cráneo [...]. Debido a esto, con la historia de *Tierra* yo le propongo la oportunidad de que vea su mundo psíquico como un absurdo del que debe alejarse [...]. La historia [...] comienza con una voz [...] que sale de la mente de Ángel, es el sonido de su angustia, la voz frágil de su existencia a la que él llama su ángel. (*65*, pp.11–12)

> Angel lives inside himself lost in the resounding cosmos of his imagination beneath the heavenly dome of his skull [...]. Because of this, in the story of *Tierra*, I provide him with the opportunity to recognise his inner world as something absurd he needs to move away from [...]. The story [...] begins with a voice [...] that comes from Ángel's mind, it is the sound of his own anguish, the fragile voice of his own existence he refers to as his angel.

A dizzying intuition of the infinite scale of the cosmos has left Ángel 'malconectado' ('badly connected') to this world and his reaction is to project the fear of his own insignificance onto an angelic *alter ego*. The contrast between the seriousness and the absurdity of Ángel's existential pretensions and his metaphysical dilemma lightens the film. Medem wanted to 'unir persona y paisaje' with 'un humor soterrado y sútil' ('link the characters to nature [in a way that was] slightly buried, subtly comic' (*30*). Rob Stone says Medem likes to watch *Tierra* laughing (*61*, p.176). Medem was particularly pleased when the film was described as 'un western metafísico' ('metaphysical Western') (*30*) and his own essay emphasizes that we are meant to find humour in Ángel's relationship to his 'angel' (*65*, p.12). The film underlines the comical side of Ángel's angelic aspirations. As the story begins, he nearly runs over a sheep so his character, first seen talking to an angel, is now ironically identified with Christ as he carries the struggling sheep on his shoulders and has a conversation with the dead shepherd, Ulloa, about life after death. The dead sheep surround Ulloa's body like four pseudo-apostles, their stiffened dead legs sticking straight up to the heavens, and the same surreal sheep are later shown peering comically out of the back of Ángel's van. Similar jokes lighten the depiction of the Patricio, who is humanized by his childlike delight in his tractor's sound system and who appears, after death, bobbing to his favourite songs. Like the earlier films, *Tierra* uses parodic images of violence to question 'macho' masculinity, again linked to male territorial competition. Violent sequences, such as the hunting of the wild boar, Patricio's burnt body winched from his tractor and the 'duel' sequence where he knocks Ángel to the ground are filmed in a comically surreal way that makes the perpetrator of the violence look foolish rather than powerful.

'Secuencia cero'

Ángel's angelic *alter ego* is an effect of his existential anxiety and an extension of the *doppelgänger* motif established in the relationship between Félix and Jota in *La ardilla*. The opening is even more distancing and paradoxical that the earlier films. The screen is black with white credits. A voice off says 'la muerte no es nada' ('death is nothing') and that human existence is always accompanied by 'un inevitable sonido de fondo, llamado angustia, que sólo soportamos a medias' ('an inevitable background noise, called anguish, that we can only half bear'). Since we can only 'half bear' it, Ángel has split himself into two. The voice continues:

> Somos una especie intrascendente rodeada de cantidades sobrecogedoras de espacio y tiempo. Un océano sin luz ni olor lo ocupa todo, excepto una partícula inmensamente pequeña [...] una isla conocida en la que vivimos, pero aún atravesada por agujeros de misterio.
>
> We are a non-transcendent species surrounded by startling quantities of space and time. An ocean, without light or smell occupies all but an immensely tiny particle [...] an island we know and on which we live, but that is still pierced by mysterious holes.

And the focus floats down from the empty black screen of the cosmos, through stars and clouds, over a patchwork of fields to home in on, then penetrate the earth, tracking through a corn field and hovering over tyre-tracks in the mud and the rain. A violent storm and single lightning-struck tree form the backdrop to the title frame: *Tierra*.

The angel's voice claims he is the part of Ángel who has died and that the person we see has 'trascendido en vida, como la cochinilla en el vino' ('has transcended in life, like the woodlouse in the wine'). This implies Ángel is a persistent but ephemeral presence on earth, like the faint taste of earth that the woodlice leave in the wine, so that this opening not only establishes what Medem has called the 'coming down to earth' of Ángel (*59*, p.12), but also his urgent need to release himself from his 'hyper-stimulated imagination'. He needs to leave his angelic *alter ego* behind and establish a less ephemeral relationship with the earth. The tracking shot from the heavens destabilizes the point of view and opens up a potentially infinite perspective, but the extreme close-ups of the woodlice reflect the way the philosophical parameters of the film narrative will be 'brought down to earth' by Ángel's 'aterrizaje' ('landing'): a landing that will also be represented ironically on two occasions when rival Patricio knocks him to the ground. Ángel's conversation with the temporarily resurrected shepherd Ulloa establishes the theme that 'la muerte no es nada' ('death is nothing') as well as the central motif of the connection between this world and the next. It also establishes the film's less serious side when one of the gypsies notes that Ulloa 'tiene cara de fiambre', ('looks like a goner'). Ulloa dies a second time and the action moves to the large white farmhouse belonging to Ángela, Patricio, Tomás and little Ángela, where the rivalry the two men will engage in is predicted in Ángel's earthly and covetous reaction to Patricio's car.

Ángel in the Community

The odd construction of the shot as Tomás opens the door shows Ángel reflected against the clouds as well as the car and the van outside, visually symbolizing the way he feels trapped between the heavens and the earth. His comment that Ángela's cooking smells good establishes her domestic credentials and the recurring theme that our sense of smell might provide an important connection with this earth. Later, Mari will be said to have a scent that attracts the wild boar at night and drives men wild, this in turn anticipates her own comment on the smell of the sea that concludes the film and illustrates the fact that Ángel has finally come down to earth. Ángel is as yet 'malconectado', however, and his sense of dislocation is represented in the boundaries and separations that recur in the narrative, emphasizing his alienation with abrupt scene changes punctuated by fades to the black screen and stars, or in sequences that show him driving along the country roads in his lonely white 'exterminator's' van. Santaolalla notes that Medem's 'narratives are as full of holes as of journeys' (*57*, p. 333) and there is repeated reference, in this as in other Basque films, to country roads as Ángel moves to and fro divided between women and between locations (*47*, pp.345–36).

Ángel is similarly 'malconectado' or disconnected from his relatives. He says he lives with his uncle, who appears only in the penultimate sequence when Ángel wakes up in hospital. The appearance of a relative connecting Ángel to the rest of the world at this late stage in the narrative could suggest the entire story up to this point has 'taken place' while he lay unconscious in his hospital bed. This in turn offers a possible way of understanding the enigmatic stone-throwing gypsy-boy, Charly, whose surreal presence in the film might be interpreted as the reaction of an unconscious Ángel to some form of medical intervention such as ECT. Ángel also tells Ángela's daughter that he has a father called Federico, but viewers who have privileged access to the 'subjective sound' of his angel know that he is an incorrigible liar (*59*, p.11). Asked where his father is, he says: 'I don't know. I've never seen him.'

Ángel's tendency to overcomplicate his life is comically contrasted with Patricio. Patricio almost shoots Ángel then says cheerfully that, had he killed him, he would just have buried him in the field and the woodlice would have disposed of the body in a couple of days so no-one would be any the wiser. The parallels and contrasts between these two men are also hinted at in the sequence where Patricio shows off his tractor. If Ángel hides somewhat anxiously beneath the 'bóveda' ('dome') of his own imagination, Patricio is happily ensconced for sixteen hours a day inside the metal 'bóveda' of this 'state-of-the-art' machine. A further parallel between the two is provided by Mari's diary in which she describes the tractor as a 'bicho' ('small animal') that she, if we can believe Ulloa, sends a thunderbolt to wipe out in a way that parallels Ángel's extermination of the smaller 'bichos', the woodlice. Ángel is associated with the legendary Basque god of thunder, Urtzi, through the name painted on the side of his van, the name of his uncle's firm of exterminators. However, appropriately enough in a narrative that parodies aggressive masculinity, it is Mari not Ángel who controls the thunderbolts that kill the Ulloa and Patricio.

Challenging traditional perspective with different points of view is a central theme in Medem's work. It was represented in the shots through the cow's eye in *Vacas* and the squirrel's point of view in *La ardilla*. Here, it is represented in the shots through the 'geoscopio' that Ángel uses to detect the woodlice and to make out the world around him. He often uses it as a telescope, noticing that the dead sheep hanging outside Ángela's house 'se está llenando de escarcha' ('is becoming filled with frost'), spotting her grandfather's attempted suicide in time to help, watching Mari and Patricio having sex in the tractor, and observing Patricio's funeral from a distance.

This odd way of perceiving the world is also represented in the surreal appearances of the old woman Cristina who brings him a glass of wine and says her own husband was called Ángel. The script suggests she should look like an elderly version of Ángela, as if personifying one of Ángel's possible futures should he stay with Ángela, but he seems a little put out when she says she is called Cristina, as if once more the connection between his imagination and the 'real' world has been revealed to be flawed.

Pursuing another possible future with a different woman, Ángel circles the isolated house Mari and Alberto share that appears in this film a little like the isolated building Ana circles in search of answers in Erice's *El espíritu de la colmena* (1973). Ángel looks at the boars' tracks, the destroyed vegetable patch and smells the sheets hanging on the line, as if he too, like the boar, is attracted by her smell, but he is nearly shot by Patricio's trap. Mari's brother, Alberto, described in the script as slightly punk hippy, arrives on his motorbike. He repeats the comment made by other characters that the 'earthy' tase of the wine doesn't bother him, laughing and declaring the rest of them to be mad ('estáis todos locos'). His amusement at the antics of humankind separates himself from the community that wants to eradicate both the woodlice and the wild boar and his opinion that they are all mad picks up Ángel's earlier comment to Ángela that he cannot understand why they want to get rid of the woodlice. Alberto's separation from the community, or rather his ability to cohabit with the earth, is also suggested in the fact that the wild boar that have decimated the vegetable garden have not touched his marijuana patch. Untroubled by the boar who are drawn to his sister, he is also untroubled by the woodlice that have infected the rest of the earth. He shows Ángel that, although they are carved out of the same local earth, there are no woodlice in the walls of his bar.

The bar is an important location for events. It is here that Patricio reminds Ángel he nearly shot him and Ángel, undeterred by his aggressive stance, takes his phone number to phone his wife, Ángela. His being torn between two women is symbolized in the fact that as he talks to Ángela he is watching Mari, who is framed by a semi-circular partition in the bar walls, like a divine incarnation in some primitive pagan cathedral. The tracking of the phone lines recalls similar shots in *Vacas* and *La ardilla*. He phones Ángela, ostensibly to say he is worried that the sheep is freezing and the tracking emphasizes the closeness of their connection, but editing destabilizes this by inserting a glimpse of him, still apparently conducting the same conversation, driving his van after Mari, and the the tracking shot comes to an end on an ominous view of the noose from which the sheep had been hanging. Romney links these shots of the phone line to Kie lowski's *Red* noting that 'these cables end unexpectedly in a dangling noose – appropriately, in a film of dazzling trickery that never stops paying out enough rope for the unwary viewer to hang themselves' (*28*).

The next phone conversation they have is more intimate: Ángel is phoning from his uncle's house in Vitoria and Ángela is recovering from food poisoning brought on by cooking and eating the dead sheep. The angel appears in the kitchen with Ángela. More information is gained about Ángel in Vitoria. He is recognized as a former patient by a man who had been a nurse in a local psychiatric hospital, and the mayor confirms the council will cover the cost of the extermination so that we next see him dressed in his white, "astronaut" suit giving out instructions to spectators and workers about the dangers of the 'aire tóxico', the poisonous gas they are about to use to kill the woodlice. Mari arrives on her motorbike and a flashback explains she and Ángel met on the road when he arrived and that it was she who encouraged him to pick up the sheep just before he met Ulloa. Sánchez Costa notes Medem's own love of speed and motorbikes and his comment that 'es curioso porque la moto la relaciono con lo hormonalmente masculino, aunque en *Tierra* sea Silke la que conduce' ('it's odd because I relate bikes, hormonally, to men, but in *Tierra* Silke rides the bike') (*13*). Mari's is a teasing presence, she calls him 'tonto' ('fool'), Ulloa's name for his sheep, and suggestions of her supernatural powers contrast with the more earthly presence of Ángela as both women are shown framing Ángel and the extermination begins. Romney describes Ángel looking 'farcically dumbfounded' framed by Ángela and Mari at the boar hunt and leads from this to the astute point that '*Tierra* is very much an ironic critique of narratives that insist on making too much sense – that rely on over-emphatic duality for their coherence' (*28*).

Male Violence

Narrative progression in *Tierra* is as enigmatic as in the earlier films. The shot of the line of exterminators is connected to the line of men with rifles chasing the wild boar via a brief interlude featuring the elderly Cristina. She offers Ángel another glass of wine and says she can feel the electricity in the air and that her teeth are freezing. Romney links her comment to Aguiresarrobe's cinematography, shot 'through a range of reddish filters that suggest the airlessness of an atmosphere thickened by electricity, as one character suggests' (*28*). This dreamlike exchange echoes Jota's comment in *La ardilla* that his teeth hurt during his near-death experience in the 'pantano' and is another reference to enigmatic otherworldly connections between this world with the next that Ángel must learn to control.

Mari arms Ángel with a rifle to shoot the boar, despite his angel's warning 'no eres hombre de sangre', ('you are not a man for blood sports' or perhaps, 'not a man of (flesh and) blood' at all?). Mari tells him to put himself between Manuel and Patricio, who are enemies. The men shout and run through the corn as if in some kind of pagan chase, reminiscent of the ones that recur in *Vacas*, and Patricio falls to the ground holding his arm and accusing the gypsy, Manuel, of shooting him. Their fight is similar to the highly stylized dream sequence where Jota and Félix fight in *La ardilla*, but in this film Manuel's son, the enigmatic stone-throwing Charly intervenes to say it was Ángel who shot Patricio. Patricio then fires a shot near Ángel's foot, causing him to jump back in the one of the literal 'fallings to earth' that function as joking asides in this narrative about a man coming down to earth. When Ángel says he doesn't mind dying, Patricio mocks him pointing out that his hands are trembling, like the 'cowardly' woodcutter Carmelo Gómez also played in *Vacas*.

This sequence ends tracking Ángel who is led away by his angel until both figures appear to fuse and the focus cuts to the bar at night. Mari is by the pool table again and the angel instructs him not to look at her provocative writhing, which is accompanied by dialogue in which Ángel admits he has been in a psychiatric hospital to have treatment for his 'hyper-stimulated' imagination. Whether he is actually seeing this vision of Mari, or whether she is just a figment of one of his more over-stimulated projections is thus left comically unclear. (Mari's diary confirms Ángel's vision of her 'outrageously serpentine body language' (*28*), but her diary is in itself a vision of Medem's, who might also be regarded as another of Ángel's *alter egos*.) The rivalry between Patricio and Ángel accelerates into a car chase that ends with Patricio threatening to put out his eyes if he catches him looking at Mari again. Here, a flashback shows Ángel watching Mari and Patricio through his 'geoscopio', then cuts back to the present where he is looking through Mari's blinds at the couple having sex. A boar sets off the trap and runs off wounded. Patricio comes out to finish it off. He also shoots out a tyre in Ángel's van and shouts that he killed the boar thinking of Ángel. The links between Ángel and the wild boar continue as Mari says provocatively through the window 'cómeme el corazon' ('eat my heart'), a line that refers back to the hunt when she told Ángel a wild boar had eaten her heart.

Ángel mistakenly accuses the gypsies of stealing when he finds the children in his van and discovers his wallet is missing. As if to defend himself he tells Manuel that he is alone ('estoy solo'), but this does not excuse a prejudice that has significant repercussions later in the story: his realization that he has maligned the gypsies takes him back to apologise which then leads to his hospitalization, bringing about the final episode in his 'coming down to earth'.

Tomás: Bridging this World and the Next

Ángel sees through his geoscope that Ángela is desperately struggling to hold up Tomás who has tried to hang himself from the noose outside their house. Having helped save his life Ángel explains, in one of his rather old-fashioned sermons, that Tomás has become separated from his wife by the age of the universe, 'veinte mil millones de años', and tells him to imagine a woodlouse. He says if

Tomás can think of the tiniest thing, he can also bridge with his thoughts the infinite distance that separates him from his wife. This dialogue expresses Ángel's own growth towards being able to live with the vast mental distance that has disconnected him from his life. He continues his lecture about coincidence and probability around the kitchen table, and his 'angel' tells Ángela how much he loves her, stepping out of Ángel's body to hug her but drawing the bodily Ángel with him so that Patricio, coming in with his daughter, is furious at this territorial imposition on his wife and throws him out of the house so that he lands with a surreal thud on the ground in another of the comic asides to male pride and the 'aterrizaje' ('coming down to earth').

Patricio's rage, observed by Ángel through his geoscope, does not subside and he shoots at the huge metal figure of the fumigator, a cartoon *alter ego* for Ángel: young Charly also throws a stone at the metal man. Left by the offended gypsies to work alone, Ángel fumigates Mari's orchard and they exchange their first declarations of 'love'. Mari's problem, she declares in a narrative we are increasingly encouraged to see as a projection of Ángel's own 'hyper-stimulated imagination', is her 'hyper-stimulated sex'. She hopes to resolve this in a relationship with Ángel, just as he hopes his imagination will be subdued by his relationship with her. Mari explains that because she is highly sexed she has never fallen in love and Ángel tells her how he is 'malconectado'. Their dialogue about their mutual need for love, like Ángel's sermons, is clichéd in a way that is both trite and ponderous at the same time. Ángel starts to spray the orchard saying he is finally calm and centred ('tranquilo y centrado') but a bottle with a message in it from Mari saying Patricio has arrived lands right at his feet disrupting this momentary peace.

Mari's Revenge?

The 'message in the bottle' marks the beginning of the rivals' final confrontation. Ángel threatenes Patricio with nozzle of his hose and sprays its poisonous fumes inside his sports car. As Ángel drives away, Patricio shoots his rifle after the van breaking one of the windows that so often framed Ángel's point of view as he looked out.

This is a visual reminder of the challenging of perspective. A surreal sequence shows the moon and clouds, fading to black with the ominous sound of the wind, lightning, a tractor, howling wind and rain, a thunderbolt, and the tractor tracks of the opening, as Ángel says 'tengo la sensación de que esto me ha pasado antes' ('I feel as if this has happened to me before'). The script confirms this, saying these repeat shots from the opening sequences, and Ángel is also quoting himself telling Manuel that he felt a sense of *déjà vu* on his arrival. This time, an ambulance cuts in front of the van instead of a sheep, because the red tractor on the top of the hill has been hit by a thunderbolt and contains the charred body of Patricio. A shot of Patricio's body in the seat from the point of view of the earthly Ángel moves to a view of his angel helping a second Patricio up onto the tractor roof and saying 'verdad que morir no es nada' ('dying's nothing, right?'). As Patricio's burnt body is winched out of the tractor, the 'angelic' Patricio remembers he does not want his daughter to see him when she gets off the school bus, and Ángel runs to find her. He tells her Patricio is dead and she comments on the blue flecks in his eyes. This oddly dissonant remark is similar to the dreamy reactions of Cristina and Peru to the horrific events of war in the woods of *Vacas*, and it is also a reminder that the image of the blue flecks in his eyes symoblize the 'otherworldly' angelic point of view from beyond life that he must learn to leave behind.

Angels Dividing

The episode at Ángela's house after Patricio's funeral marks a turning point. Tomás is happy because Ángel has helped him 'find' his wife again. Ángela is selling the car Ángel coveted to Alberto. She asks him if he shot Patricio and Ángel explains that he is complex being, half angel, half man, but that he thinks it was his angel who shot Patricio because he was in love with her. He says to his angel that he is getting better, and to Ángela that he would not be surprised if his angel stayed with her. He then tells them he feels less dead every day. The focus cuts to an enigmatic long shot of Ángel fumigating the three remaining now half skeletal sheep. He repeats that he has got rid of the taste of earth for one year and, over a shot of the metal fumigator dented by Patricio's shots and Charly's stone, his voice-off says he will celebrate the fact that he, rather than the woodlice, has 'trascendido'. After this, the focus cuts to the final sequence in the bar where he talks of leaving for Portugal and Mari plays pool with Manuel. Ángela arrives, dressed up in the hope of attracting Ángel, and the angel sits next to her. Ángela says the first thing she noticed about Ángel was the blue flecks in his eyes which Ángel claims are not his (they are a symbolic reflection of his angel's vision through his own eyes). Despite his angel's wish that he stay with Ángela he follows Mari home.

Tierra sets up archetypal misogynist stereotypes as the projection of male fantasy, or mental ill-health, then confuses and blurs them. Ángel spends a night of non-orgasmic passion with Mari that is supposed to cure her of her nymphomania, then offers to take her with him to Portugal. Telling himself he is going to stop being complicated, he immediately complicates the situation by having sex with 'virtuous mother' Ángela in the shower. At an awkward breakfast, Ángel lectures them about the brain saying it contains 'un universo de diez mil millones de neuronas, y mil billones de circuitos' and that it hides 'un océano negro, desconocido [...] Pero es generador de desorden' ('a universe of a ten thousand million neurons and a thousand billion circuits [...] a black unknown ocean [...] it generates disorder'). In the silence that occurs when Ángela asks whether Ángel or Alberto will drive her home, Ángel sees his own reflection in the coffee and offers to go. His face reflected against the black coffee is another visual reference to the 'océano negro' he has just described, as if his growing ability to adjust his sense of dislocation to the parameters of the cosmos is illustrated in the confinement of that ocean to the rim of a cup of coffee.

Ángela finds the wallet he accused the gypsies of stealing in the van, and Ángel, who has just upset Mari, now rejects Ángela as well. He goes to apologise to Charly, but Charly hits him with a stone, knocking him to the ground. The figure of Patricio appears dancing by the tractor and Ángel tells Charly not to worry, that if he dies he can bury him under the tractor. He is paraphrasing Patricio's earlier comment about burying Ángel in order not to complicate his life when he says to them 'no quiero arruinaros la vida' ('I don't want to ruin your lives'). A fade to the cosmic blackness opens onto Ángel in a white hospital gown like Sofía in *La ardilla*, who was also in the process of leaving a part of her identity behind. His uncle, sitting on the bed, asks how he feels, and he replies, now paraphrasing Ulloa instead of Patricio, 'crujiente como recién llegado' ('crunchy, as if I'd only just arrived'). His uncle says a very pretty woman has been looking after him, then laughs when Ángel asks, 'rubia o roja' ('blonde or redhead?'). Mari appears and they agree to travel far away together. The script explains, where the film does not, that Ángela pushes her into the ward and stays behind with Alberto. The film denies viewers this more positive ending for Ángela as the focus cuts to the invisible angel accompanying her and her daughter across a field. After another cut to the black cosmos the sea appears and Mari makes her final comment: '¡Qué bien huele el mar! ¡No hay nada major!' as the white van exits a frame then filled by flocks of birds and the dedication to Meden's son, Peru.

Conclusion

Mari's comment is wonderfully mundane, deflating this narrative of metaphysical inquiry for the last time. The question why the woodlice should affect the taste of the wine is not answered because it represents the wider unanswerable questions about the meaning of life and death that haunt Ángel. Even as the film is reaching its conclusion Ángel says the mystery of the woodlice has yet to be solved. The former psychiatric nurse who had recognized Ángel as a patient, notes they breed in the cemetery, to which the Mayor replies that they clearly cannot fumigate there, but this suggestion that the woodlice might represent a heaven-sent plague is really just another *non-sequitur*. Ángel says the next harvest will be normal but they will be back the following year, so the mayor's conclusion is 'no hemos adelantado gran cosa' ('we haven't got very far').

Tierra is an existential enigma, agoraphobic in its fear of cosmic space and riddled with elusive motifs. Ángel is split between his imaginary angel and himself, and he projects these inner divisions onto the female characters. Medem claims he finds salvation in the choice between two women (*65*, p.14), and that he chooses Mari because she is 'más terrena y primaria' ('more earthly, more primary') and therefore requires 'toda la presencia de Ángel hombre' ('all the presence of Ángel the man', *65*, p.14). The theme of love divided, represented in *Vacas* when Ignacio chooses Catalina over Magdalem and in *La ardilla* when Sofía chooses Jota over Félix, is expressed here by the representation of two opposed women (leather-clad nymphomaniac versus virtuous mother) who are so stereotypical they can only really be excused as figments of Angel's 'hiperexcitada imaginación'. At the end of the film, the quest for identity concludes with Mari's wonderfully simple statement and Ángel is brought 'down to earth' by female objects of desire that are represented as projections of his divided personality. In spite of the central theme of existential angst, the emphasis is on the mundane rather than the metaphysical. Medem says the film is 'anti-religious, anti-Catholic' (*5*, p.14). The empty religious iconography (the dead shepherd, the protagonist with a struggling lamb on his shoulders and his guiding angel) combine with the clues that the world of *Tierra* exists only inside Ángel's head to suggest that these 'other-worldly', religious motifs are merely the grandiose projections of his mental disorder. Despite the repetition of the 'angelic' names, *Tierra* does not suggest there is any form of transcendence to be found in Christian iconography. Ángel chooses not 'good mother' Ángela but Mari, whose name links her to a pagan goddess of sexuality and retribution.

Stone notes that it is difficult always to know when to take Medem seriously (*61*, p.176) and is cautious about an ending that 'disappoints because it is based upon the objectionable male fantasy of dividing the compliant female into angel and whore' (*61*, p.175). Derek Elley's review of the film is amusingly damning: 'Basque *wunderkind* Julio Medem's long-awaited third feature is a sumptuously attired, cosmic love story that rattles like an empty can.' He says it 'boils down to the story of a confused guy torn between two opposite women – homely, 30ish Angela and sex-on-legs teenager Mari' and dismisses the film as 'at best murky metaphysics, at worst, cosmic claptrap'. He is particularly unamused by Ángel's *alter ego*: 'The question of whether Angel is in fact an angel in human form is left dangling like one of the charred sheep' and concludes that 'Gómez [...] makes a handsome but finally rather wimpy hero, hard to fathom as the love object of two striking femmes' (*25*).

Medem says the cosmos and the underground world of the woodlice exist only in Ángel's imagination and that the film is meant to mock his sense of his own complexity (*65*, pp.11–12). He also explains that Ángel over-interprets conversations and daily events in order to compensate for his own sense of inferiority (*65*, p.14) He makes unlikely connections, such as the fact that Ángela's teacher, Federico, may be the father he has never met, in order to be able to imagine some kind of 'conexión cósmica' between random events and coincidences (*65*, p.14). Although he says it is typically human, in the face of our cosmic insignificance, to 'sobrevalorarse con la trascendencia' ('overvalue notions of our transcendence') (*65*, p.14), he wonders if the secret to life is to 'adaptar la pequeñez humana, aferrarse a la *Tierra* y disfrutar de la seducción de todas las formas de misterio' ('adapt to our human smallness, cling to the earth and enjoy the seductive aspects of all forms of mystery') (*65*, p.15). He concludes that 'to say that life is simple you need a complex film' (*5*, p.14). In this way Medem updates what came to be know as 'Pascal's Wager' for a secular age. The wager was that it is better to have faith in God because, should He exist, there is more to be gained by believing than not. The distance between human beings and the cosmos that Pascal suggests we bridge with faith in God is visually illustrated in *Tierra* by shots of the black screen that stand in for the idea of infinite space, but Medem updates Pascal's aphorism by using Ángel's journey to illustrate an alternative wager that, should there be nothing beyond this world, there is more to be gained by placing our feet firmly on its surface while we are here.

It was with reference to this film that Medem told Paul Julian Smith 'the film doesn't belong to me, it belongs to whoever sees it' (*5*, p.14), and I want to end here with a personal interpretation from Medem's own father. Apparently he had one minor criticism of *Tierra* which was that he thought that between Charly throwing the stone and Ángel waking up in hospital the dissolve to black was held too long so the audience thought Ángel had died and was then shocked to find he was still alive (*44*, pp.231–32). Medem did not change the editing but he says when the film was finally shown at Cannes, a year late after the delay caused by Banderas, it was the week after his father died. He describes how, watching it again on a big screen he agreed with his father, it was too long. He says this was the last thing he learnt from his father and his next film *Los amantes de círculo polar*, the final film examined in this guide is dedicated to his memory.

4. *Los amantes del Círculo Polar:* Symphony in White[12]

'Estoy esperando la casualidad de mi vida'
'I'm waiting for the coincidence of my life'

Synopsis

Otto and Ana meet outside their school in 1980. Otto is running after a football and Ana is running away from news of her father's death. Otto's father, Álvaro, tells him he is leaving his German mother and Otto launches a flotilla of paper aeroplanes with a fundamental, but never explained, question about love from the window of the school toilets. Ana picks one up and gives it to her mother, Olga, claiming Otto's father wrote the question. Her wish to get closer to Otto is motivated by her superstitious belief that, because he appeared on the day her father died, her father is 'speaking' to her through Otto. Otto's paper plane and Ana's lie bring about a relationship between the parents and Otto falls in love with Ana. Otto moves in with his

[12] This is an adaptation of the title of Javier Hernández Ruiz's review, 'Symphony of Spheres' (*31*, p.30).

stepfamily and we learn he was named after a German pilot, who became trapped in a tree after parachuting out of his plane the day Guernica was bombed, 26 April 1937. Otto runs away when his mother commits suicide. Olga has met a German, Álvaro Midelman, who offers her a job as a newsreader, so that, in another of the films many odd coincidences, she reads the news about the German President apologising to the Basque people for the bombing of Guernica.

The step-family breaks up and Otto and Ana do not meet again. Ana has a relationship with Otto's former teacher, and Otto becomes a pilot delivering mail. Olga and Álvaro leave for Australia and Ana leaves for Álvaro's father's cabin in Finland. Ana sends, care of his father, a letter to Otto that Otto himself flies to Madrid, explaining she has met his namesake who married a Spaniard, Cristina, and left the German army. She is living in their cabin on the edge of the Arctic Circle. Ana waits for Otto on the day of the summer solstice, when the sun never sets, and Otto throws himself out of his plane in a parachute that gets caught in a tree only metres from where Ana is waiting. Hearing that a messenger plane has crashed in the north of Finland Ana gets a lift into town to find out whether Otto was on it. In the final section Ana is knocked over by a bus, but is also shown running up to German Otto's flat where she is reunited with her own Otto, who is waiting for her in the kitchen. At the same time Otto, rescued from the tree by a polite Finn, follows Ana into town, but arrives to find her dying at the side of the road, having been knocked over by a bus. The final shots of Otto's reflection in Ana's eyes and a return to the crashed plane, convey the further possibility that both are dead and that the events following from his crash-landing in the tree are as much an illusion as the images of Ana running upstairs to Otto.

Analysis

After the breakdown of his marriage and death of his father, Medem turned down the offer to direct *Zorro* and went instead to stay in his brother's flat in Paris to concentrate on writing the film he would dedicate to his father (*61*, p.176). Medem describes it as 'una historia de amor en estado puro' ('a film about love in its pure state') (*11*, p.45). It was inspired in part by a short story by Ray Loriga (*35*, p.82; *61*, p.177) but it also develops the themes of earlier works: war and history, the blurring of fantasy and reality, love and the family, destiny and chance, nature, life and death, and the alternating points of view proposed by Mari's diary in *Tierra*. Among these chance and destiny are central. Ana refers repeatedly to 'casualidad' ('coincidence', or 'chance') and Medem calls it one of the 'motores íntimos' of the film (*44*, p.235). The element of chance relationships has additional meaning for Medem as there was an unexpected twist to the story of the girl he fell in love with in his teens. She was discovered to be the granddaughter of an illegitimate daughter of Medem's great grandfather. When this was realised the two families met up and joked about the new 'ramo bastardo' ('bastard line'), and Medem comments that 'fue nuestro lugar común de aterrizaje, en el que se desvelaron todos los secretos' ('it was our own communal coming down to earth, when all the secrets were revealed') (*44*, p.235). Secrets, odd chance relationships and historical coincidences also structure the 'aterrizaje' of *Los amantes*.

Before its release Medem said he thought this film was his most direct one so far and that viewers would find it easy to respond to (*11*, p.45). It is easier to follow than *Tierra*, but it is not straightforward, and its abstract visual and narrative patterns inspired Romney's comment that Medem may be 'cinema's last full-blown symbolist' (*36*, p.48). *Los amantes* returns the dual point of view envisaged for *Tierra* and was also Medem's first non-linear script. The first sequences begin in the 'present' in Finland as the voiceovers of Otto or Ana respectively comment on the past, while the six different actors move the action forwards to the opening and closing moments. The names, Otto and Ana, are palindromes, like Medem. They have personal connections: Medem's father's brother, Otto, was a pilot in Franco's 'Blue Division' who fought against the Russians during the Second World War, one of his brothers is Álvaro, and his sister, who sadly died during the filming of *Los amantes*, was called Ana (*39*, p.270), but they also have a formal function. They can be read, like the film narrative, forwards and backwards. The palindromes are the 'mystery' in this film that in *Tierra* was why the woodlice make the wine taste of earth, in *La ardilla* was the 'mystery' of romantic love, and in *Vacas* was symbolised by the hollow tree stump.

Los amantes was always planned as a parallel story and Medem wrote it as we see it on-screen. He claims he was only really sure where the story was going when the step-siblings kiss while looking at the map of the Arctic Circle (*44*, p.237), but the location had already been inspired by the 'Festival of the Midnight Sun' (*61*, p.178). Medem had attended the festival near Rovaniemi, the administrative capital of Lapland in Finland, six years earlier for a screening of *Vacas*. He met Aki Kaurismäki there, a director Medem admired and to whom he pays homage in the character of Aki who helps Otto down from the tree (*44*, p.239).

Unlike *Vacas*, in which the same actors play different characters, this film needed different actors to play the same characters. Medem had seen Fele Martínez in *Tesis* (Amenábar, 1996) and was drawn to him at the Goya Awards (the Spanish version of the Oscars) for 'el aspecto romántico que le daba el pel rubio' ('romantic look of his blond hair') (*8*). This is a new departure as the male protagonists of the earlier films tend to be dark like Medem. The youngest Otto is played by Medem's son Peru (*44*, p.242–3). Najwa Nimri, whom Medem had seen in Calparsoro's *Salto al vacío* (1995), was always intended for Ana, but it took some time to find the adolescent Ana. Sixteen year old Kristel Díaz (who plays her between Nimri and Sara Valiente) has blue eyes which had to be disguised. This is a small but somehow fitting detail with reference to a director who has made the blue in brown eyes something of a recurring motif (*44*, p.243). Heredero opens his analysis of *Los amantes* with reference to the 'ojos azules que se enredan' ('tangled blue eyes') of *La ardilla* and the flecks of blue in Ángel's eyes. He then notes *Los amantes*, which opens with the reflection of Otto in Ana's eyes, is 'toda ella bañada en azules' ('all bathed in blues') (*39*, pp.267–68). Symbolically, the tangled blue in *La ardilla* stood for lost love and the flecks of blue in *Tierra* for death, both of which are fundamental to this love story. The effect of being 'bathed in blues' was provided by cinematographer Kalo

Berrido, who worked on Medem's short films and on *La ardilla* and brought this film the colder, harder quality Medem wanted, unlike the rich reds Medem praises Aguirresarobe for contributing to *Tierra* (*44*, p.217).[13]

'Secuencia cero'

Time pressures meant the episodes filmed in Finland had to be shot first to catch the midnight sun and Medem says that to begin by filming the lovers' tragic end was difficult psychologically for him and for the actors (*44*, p.245). The screenplay also begins at the end with a mesmerisingly cryptic and melancholic sequence. The song that accompanies the white screen, black credits and snow blends with the sound of the wind into Iglesias's haunting sound track. Like the tractor tracks in *Tierra*, obscure shapes in the snow reveal themselves only gradually to be the debris from a plane crash. A newspaper with a photograph of the crashed plane blows in the wind, which has always been an ominous motif in Medem's films. There is a young woman's face, her boots as she runs and a young man chases her, she runs up to the old man's flat and the couple hug. Then there is the iconic shot of the extreme close up of the women's eyes, her partner's face reflected in her pupils. A fade to white concludes the credit sequence, and the word 'Otto' establishing the initial point of view.

Otto

The story begins with the aerial perspective of Otto flying over Finland. His statement that it is a good thing lives have various circles, but that his has a single unfinished one predicts the tragic outcome and also describes the central motif of the circles that has just been inscribed visually by the vision of him in Ana's eyes. The events that follow are memories as he flies over Finland, checks his

---

[13] The links to Kieslowski's *Trois couleurs* trilogy (1993, 1994, 1994)) have been noted (*53*), and Medem used *Trois couleurs: bleu* as a reference for his cinematographer (*44*, p.243). Via Rivera also notes the influence of Resnais's *L'Année dernière à Marienbad* (1961) (*62*, p.212).

petrol gage and wonders about Ana, and the mixture of intense emotion and gently comic abstraction they convey sets the tone.

Of the day he first met Ana he says: 'De niño vivía rodeado del resto del mundo, me sentía protegido, hasta que una tarde de frío, a la salida del colegio, pasó algo…' ('As a child I lived surrounded by the rest of the world, I felt protected, until one cold afternoon coming out of school, something happened…'). His sense of security ends when his father says he is divorcing his mother on the day he meets Ana as he follows the flight of the (circular) football kicked from the school yard. A fade to white cuts to Anna running in front of him in her red tights and woolly hat. The fades to white that punctuate this film contrast with the fades to black in *Tierra* that symbolised the terrifying 'espaces infinis'. Here, they symbolise the fear of 'love running out' that is reflected in the wintry *mise-en-scène* Kalo Berridi achieved with a blue gelatine filter (*44*, p.243) and that Stone notes is a counterbalance to the lovers' passion (*61*, p.179). Ana falls and Otto's adult narrative voiceover asks 'Where do girls run to?' and 'Why is she looking at me like that?

In Medem's films the chasm that divides the sexes also attracts. Their mutual strangeness to one another is symbolised in recurrent motifs of separation, distance or mystery such as the fern grove in *Vacas*, the fundamental lie in *La ardilla* and the stereotypical split projections of the women in *Tierra*. The social conditioning that enhances the division is represented in the strict gender-segregation of the classroom, the girls taught by a woman, the boys by a man. Otto asks his teacher whether girls ask the same questions as boys. The boys cheer when their teacher says they don't ask so many, but are dashed when he says that is because girls their age are older than them. For the beginning of this representation of Medem's closest and most divided of lovers Otto's rhetorical questions convey a sense of bewildered intrigue. Like Ángel in his conversations over the kitchen table, Otto reflects on the extraordinary chance of their meeting: what would have happened if the ball had been kicked earlier, he saved the goal, and everyone had congratulated him? That the course of his life might have been altered by a heroic sporting moment is another comic reflection of mixed-up modern masculinity, like the slo-mo (re)action shot in *La ardilla*. The link set up between running (after the ball) and desire (for Ana) echoes the chases through the wood in *Vacas*, the race for Sofía, and the hunt for wild boar in *Tierra*.

The first two opening sequences establish the profound loss that changes the lives of the children. Medem describes how first love made him feel alone and unprotected (*44*, p. 235). Otto loses his security, by chance, on the day he runs after the ball. This is established with a powerful sequence of abruptly edited images that combine to form a visual shorthand version of events. The sequence presents a startling balance of tragedy and comedy: cutting abruptly from his vision of Ana to the car, Otto's discussion with his father moves all too rapidly from the weather to divorce. The weather is metaphorical: Álvaro likes the cold, Otto likes summer. Álvaro explains everything has a cycle and everything dies (at which point there is an insert shot of his mother cleaning lettuce). Everything runs out in the end, like the petrol in the tank says Álvaro, and a close up of their faces cuts to an extreme close up of a petrol gage registering empty that dissolves into a flashback to a 2CV and his mother saying: 'It can't last for ever, you have to accept the good and the bad.' His father is flagging down a red car, and driving off with another woman, jauntily waving the spare petrol can out of the window, when the focus cuts returns to the 'present' where young Otto slaps his father in the face for nearly crashing into a red bus and his father asks for forgiveness, saying it is not his fault and that he is leaving Otto's mother. Otto's grief is now symbolised by the empty tank and the red bus. The bus and the petrol tank are metaphors of loss that direct the narrative, like the white cow in *Vacas*. Cutting abruptly forward to a night scene, the shot of the window blowing open at night in the rain is another visual motif related to the guilt that will haunt Otto in relation to his mother. Otto tells her he will always love her and that if the petrol runs out he will die, then the focus cuts back to the present, tracking along the plane, an aerial shot of Finland, a river, the fuel gage, and Otto's question: 'How will this journey end?'

Otto's first section also includes the visually stunning sequence with the flying paper aeroplanes, launched with his unexplained question about love, from the bathroom window of the school. One nearly gets caught on the high gate but falls, finally, into the girls' yard. Flying and landing are constant motifs in Medem's films: the flying woodchip in *Vacas*, Sofía thrown from the sky in *La ardilla* and Ángel's existential 'landing' in *Tierra*. Here, the trajectory of the ball is retraced and dispersed by innumerable paper planes, one of which Ana will use to bring the parents, herself and this strange boy together. Fele Martínez describes Otto as 'un enamorado del amor, de su esencia pura' ('in love with love, with its pure essence') (*35*, p.83) and Ana describes the question about love that we never see as 'la pregunta de toda la vida' ('the question of a lifetime'). At another home time, Otto stubbornly waits in the rain while his father shouts at him from the car. Otto wants to introduce himself to Ana. He is closing and opening his eyes like camera shutters and like Ana in Saura's *Cría cuervos* (1975) trying to conjure up her dead mother. Giving up, he runs to the car to find Ana already there in the back so it she who introduces herself to him.

Medem has said his fundamental concern is with emotion (*40*, p.62), and the abstract formalism, the stark quality of these abruptly edited sequences heightens the emotion and development of the themes of loss and guilt. As with poems, the control of form condenses and intensifies the impact of the content of the imagery. Editing imitates the kaleidoscopic structure of Otto's memory. This is an emotional, not an empirical version of events, so it can be motivated by surreal coincidences, such as repeated near accidents between a car and a red bus.

Ana

Ana's first section answers at least one of Otto's rhetorical questions. She is looking at Otto 'like that' because she sees him as her dead father. The sequence opens again in Finland, Ana's waiting established with a long shot of the sun and the lake with the rock in it. She is waiting near the cabin bisected by the Arctic Circle, the line of it painted across the floor once again gesturing to the formal precision of the narrative. She says she will stay as long as possible, waiting for the 'la casualidad de la vida' the biggest coincidence in a life that is has been a sequence of coincidences. Najwa Nimri describes Ana as the victim of a life that has dealt her a 'desencuentro gigantesco' ('huge separation') (*35*, p.83). Her story cuts back to the same point in time as Otto's. Her mother is waiting for her at the school gate in dark glasses. Ana backs away before her mother can speak. She runs from her mother, the adult voiceover explains, to hold on to her father's life. She feels if she stops he will 'fall', but it is she who falls.

Her fall coincides with Otto's appearance so she decides he is a manifestation of her father, despite the fact that he looks nothing like old photos of her father. The irrelevance of Otto's looks is noteworthy in a film about the importance of point of view. An insert shot of a car overtaking a lorry, the close up of an empty petrol gauge, then an on-coming car accompany Ana's question about how her father died. Again, there are echoes from earlier films in the image of falling and the car crash: Begoña lost her German husband in a car crash and tried to replace him with an 'Otto'; Félix and Sofía's accidents were also associated respectively with the desperate search for, and flight from, love.

Ana picks up one of the paper planes and says she loves the cold, as if unconsciously contributing to Otto and Álvaro's conversation in the car. She gives the paper to her mother and claims Otto's father 'sent' it. Both parents are dressed in black and white according to the minimal arctic colour palate of the film, and perhaps to the 'black and white' simplicity of Ana's interpretation of the world at this point in time. Ana sees the paper plane as a message from her father through Otto. The children's parents introduce themselves as Olga and Álvaro. Cutting to the day it rains and Otto gets into the car, drenched, the children are shot awkwardly from above in a way that brings to mind Santaolalla's astute comment about Medem's 'worlds which are located "at a slight angle" to reality' (*57*, p.334). They find they share names that are 'capicúas' ('palindromes'), which Ana's older voiceover claims her father said brought good luck. Ana feels dizzy, confused by the fact that her father is not speaking through Otto quite in the way she would like, but she decides Otto speaks on the outside and her father on the inside, in a way that echoes the doubling of Ángel conveyed through the movements, or not, of the actor's lips in *Tierra*. The concluding event in Ana's first section confirms her stubborn belief in spite of evidence to the contrary: she asks her father to blow her a kiss if he can hear her, and from his mother's doorstep young Otto blows her a kiss.

Otto

Taking up where Ana's sequence left off, Otto's voiceover explains he was so in love with Ana he didn't wonder why she was so strange. Passing time is indicated in the artificial and quaint wipes that move through the different journeys from school. Hernández Ruiz praises the 'foco corto que aplasta los fondos y enmarca los personajes encerrados en su propio drama amoroso' ('shortened focus that flattens depth and marks the characters imprisoned in the drama of their love') (*31*, p.31). Ana stares at Otto silently and when Olga asks why they don't talk like brother and sister, both vehemently reject the idea, although the parents are moving into a new house together. Jonathan Romney notes that 'this is an intensely edited film, with emphasis on staggering leaps: a lurching car in a near-miss accident abruptly vaults the narrative several years into the future' (*36*, p.48). Otto's adult voiceover introduces such a vault here saying that 'changes come all of a sudden' as another bus appears and Olga nearly crashes into it. As Otto and Ana jerk backwards into their seats again the children have been replaced by the teenager actors.

Olga remonstrates with the bus driver; Otto is transfixed by Ana's thigh. Olga slaps the bus driver in the face, gets back in and says they are old enough to get the bus. Focus cuts to Otto alone in a bus as the voiceover explains he now only saw Ana every other weekend. This sequence repeats the earlier one with the near crash, the slapped face and the irrevocable event: Otto will leave his mother to see Ana more often and his mother will commit suicide, as a result, he thinks, of his betrayal. Cutting to Otto walking around the outside, significantly, of the new 'family' home, on the inside we see mildly comical shots of the new 'family man' Álvaro, with his more conventional short hair, setting the table and kissing his wife. Otto moves around to look into Ana's bedroom and the voiceover explains he wanted to tell Ana he loved her, but his face is reflected in the opaque transparency of the window that she opens without seeing him, visually symbolising that she cannot see him because she is still looking through him to her father.

Ana

This section establishes a link between love and war as well as the first part of the most important narrative loop concerning 'Otto, el piloto'. To the sound of bombs, Ana's voiceover explains her father took some time to leave Otto, which is an endearing way of saying she gradually stopped projecting her grief onto him and was then able to listen to him. Significantly, what she hears is the story of the bombing of Guernica and the story about Otto's name. The day the Basque town of Guernica was bombed by Germans, Otto's grandfather helped a German pilot, Otto, who had parachuted into a tree, and the men shared a cigarette. In the flashback 'Álvaro' plays the grandfather and the German is another of Medem's astronaut-like 'fallen angels'. When Álvaro fell in love with a German woman, his father said she was a gift from his friend Otto, so they named Otto after him. Olga wonders why anyone would name a child after a Nazi, or indeed save a Nazi's life. Her 'black and white', prosaic deflation of the story that is so poetic for the lovers reinforces the distance between the children and the parents. Medem also reflects this distance formally, saying they were 'filmed in such a way that the kids practically turn their back on their parents, filming them either from in front or behind. If the parents are there, they're out of focus' (*61*, p.179). This brief section closes with Ana's comment that she would like to be in love too.

Otto

The sound of the plane and the aerial view of the river and close up of the map in the 'present' provide a visual bridge back to past where Ana is telling Otto about the midnight sun and the Arctic Circle. Medem says the film is about two lonely people who 'invent the Polar Circle' as a safe place to meet (*44*, p.235). Otto's frustration is represented, comically, by the insert shot of a large reindeer bellowing, and Ana kisses him. The action cuts to the day Otto moves into this 'family' home with its cool blue tones and blue sitting room walls. The close-up of the phone line echoes the phone line that tracked towards Ángela, the rejected woman in *Tierra*. Otto says he will see his mother every day after school, but the transfer of loyalties that will later induce such guilt in him is framed in another of Medem's staged family photos.

In *Vacas*, the irony of the staged family photo was underscored by the presence of the illegitimate Peru; in this staging a similar effect is provided by the passing of the note with the invitation 'salta por la ventana valiente' ('be brave, jump through the window') and the night when Otto is shown going into Ana's room twice, in a sequence which has visual echoes of the opening and closing window in Otto's bedroom at his mother's house. The association made by the chiaroscuro lighting, the wind and the shadows on the wall combines with the subsequent episode in which Otto discovers his mother's body. This night sequence is a visual premonition of the guilt Otto will come to feel for the way his desire for Ana led him to 'betray' the mother he said he would never stop loving. At his mother's flat, the discovery of her body is filmed using both the adult and child actors to represent Otto's instinctive regression away from the discovery. The wind bangs a door, the surreal single fly crosses the frame and Otto sniffs in the corridor, the wind blowing his hair. Smelling was also about trying to fathom the unfathomable in *Tierra*, but there the mystery was Mari's magnetic attraction. Here it is the presence of death. The earlier insert shot of his mother cleaning lettuce is explained by the flies on the rotting lettuce glimpsed through the gap in the door, and when he does finally open the door the doubling of adult and child Ottos concludes with the reaction shot of the adult Otto jerking backwards and setting off his camera by mistake.

This inappropriate taking of a picture cuts abruptly to the contrastingly idyllic memory of his younger self taking the photo of his mother in her white bathing suit by the lake near a mountain. In this idealised sequence his mother is defending his father and Otto says she can only do that because she still loves him. The photo and the comment will recur. His mother replies that a mother's love lasts for life time, and the focus cuts to her coffin and the white corridors of what seems to be a cross between a mortuary and a crematorium. Otto's grief is established in the odd location and the awkward angles. The actors are foreshortened as if through the concave window (another circle that echoes not only the circles that confine the narrative, but also the circle of the camera lens that confines its form and frames the actors, like the 'juke box' shots that frame Sofía in *La ardilla*). The row that follows will be represented slightly differently from Ana's point of view, but Olga's comment that he is 'demasiado orgulloso' ('too proud') is something she later says also to Ana. Otto's face is shot through the circle as the coffin disappears and editing cuts to a coffin in flames. The screen fades to white, and to a winter scene of snow and trees.

Otto and Ana are on an old-fashioned wooden sled, heading for the edge of a cliff. Álvaro shouts at them and Ana jumps off but Otto doesn't stop. His surreal fall and crash, explained by his comment that he wanted to be with his mother, leads into the dream sequence that loops back to the original German Otto and forward to the Arctic Circle when the bear-like man in furs skis upwards with Otto on his back. This section concludes with Otto's vision of a log fire, a Finnish cabin, Ana arriving and Otto asking if she wants to be his mother.

Ana

Returning to the sequence where they first kiss and the photograph of the reindeer that is now an emblem of Otto's frustrated love, Ana's voiceover makes cryptic reference to the bellowing reindeer when she notes it is hard to fall in love because you not only have to want it, you have to hear it. Her view of events is markedly different because it is not tainted by the guilt that threatens to destroy Otto. As Marian Via Rivera notes, the games Otto and Ana invent become a way of trying to impose an illusory order on events (*62*, p.205). They spy voyeuristically on their parents and Ana explains she came as close as she could to being able to love Otto in the way he loved her, but her version is playful. Teenage Ana becomes Najwa Nimri, the adult Ana, teasing her mother with the disappearing acts of that 'bicho raro de tu hijo' ('strange creature your son'), as Olga refers to Otto.

Ana's comment that her heart has never again been 'so red' is the verbal bridge to the sequence in the shop where Otto, still teasing Olga, dithers over the red leather hearts and Olga meets her second Álvaro, Álvaro Midelman. His name is a joking reference to his function as a go-between for the lovers and for the two Ottos. Vicente Molina Foix mentions his comic and inexplicable arrival as an example of an adept changing of tempo 'cuando la temperatura sube demasiado' ('when the temperature goes up too far') that introduces the way the television becomes a kind of comic motif in the film (*34*, p.23). Olga, the woman who could not understand why anyone would name a child after a 'Nazi', becomes the newsreader who announces the German president's apology to the Basque people for the killing of civilians at Guernica. As she reads the news, Otto has his hand on her daughter's leg. Romney notes that 'the only explicitly Basque factor is the reference to Guernica, which allows for a multiple flourish of taboo-busting: not-quite siblings Ana and Otto neck on the sofa, as her mother on television reads a news item about German reparations for the bombing. The scene supplies more grist to the film's already complex incestuous thematics and it's only appropriate, after all, that a film about quasi-incestuous passion should be this audaciously, self-devouringly involuted' (*36*, p.48)

Editing cuts abruptly to the scene where they will surprise Olga and her German Álvaro and Otto runs inside the Finnish Travel Agent to hide. From Olga's bluffing to her daughter that nothing is going on, Ana's voiceover cuts to fact that Otto never recovered from his mother's death and to her own recollection of the strange, surreal sequence in the white corridor that shows Otto screaming and throwing himself bodily across the corridor, and a fade into his attempted suicide on the sled. 'Otto wanted to die' says the older voiceover, 'and I went with him'. According to her memory, she did not jump but was pulled off the sledge by Álvaro. In her determination to find him she staggers, waist-deep through the snow, is nearly hit by the sled falling from the tree, and says, echoing the superstitious girl who ran from her father's death: 'You aren't dead so I'm not going to cry'. Her voiceover concludes that Otto's guilt over his mother's suicide was so great that it encircled her too, and her section closes with Otto leaving home.

Olga is looking for the missing Otto again, and there is painful irony in her assumption that Ana is being facetious when she says Otto didn't sleep with her. Ana's sense of loss when she realises he has gone this time is reflected in the way she places herself, almost bodily, inside his near-empty wardrobe as if it might hold the key to his disappearance. Heredero describes *Los amantes* as 'un hermoso cuento de hadas que es también un valioso exorcismo personal, un bello poema de amor y de muerte' ('a beautiful fairytale that is also a personal exorcism and a beautiful poem about love and death') (*39*, p.272). Bearing in mind the fairytale quality and the recurrent fades to white it is perhaps not too fanciful to see echoes in this of C.S.Lewis's wardrobe that links to a wintry landscape in which a boy will lose his heart, as well as to the arctic landscapes that freeze Kay's heart in Hans Christian Andersen's *Snow Queen*.

Otto/Ana

A shot of the flowery wall paper of Otto's rented room and another high angle anticipating his aerial point of view introduce the sequence that establishes the lovers' separation contrasted formally in the 'joining together' of their recollections: the abrupt jumps from Otto to Ana, and from one timescale to the next represent their dislocation. Otto places the symbolic photograph of his mother by his, also symbolic, metal-framed single bed, and the focus zooms to the red leather heart he places next to it, and cuts to Ana looking at her own red heart. The step-siblings' secret is out and the *mise-en-scène* confirms the irrevocable barriers that divide the step-family. Olga shouts at Ana to open her door. Ana's voiceover says Otto stole money from his father (who is shown sitting alone in the garden), as she closes her wooden shutters against Olga who wants to send her to a psychiatrist. A dissolve to blurred shots of Otto banging himself bodily against the flowery walls of his room fade to white and cut to the sequence at the Plaza Mayor where the lovers so narrowly miss one another. This sequence was described by Heredero as 'sorprendentemente torpe' ('surprisingly clumsy') (*39*, p.271), but Marina Via Rivera is more sympathetic. She notes 'there is a reason for Otto and Ana's blindness in the Plaza Mayor, as there must also be a reason why we never learn what is 'la pregunta de amor, demasiado bonita para la letra de un niño' [...]. We never see the message since, in my view, it is one of the film's many blind spots. The blind spot itself triggers the start of the game, and therefore of the entrance into the labyrinth' (*62*, p.209). The 'game' begins when Ana meets Otto's former teacher, and Otto circles the job advert that will turn him into a messenger and allow him to recreate the persona of his namesake, 'Otto el piloto'. Ana remarks on the coincidence of meeting Otto's old teacher, but says there are no good coincidences any more, and that it is her fault because she spent them too soon. Otto passes them as his former school teacher recognises Ana is Otto's sister.

The rest of this section presents the repercussions of Otto's departure. An abruptly aged Álvaro opens the door to Otto, wearing black and white. He slaps Otto across the face and accuses him destroying his life. His bitterness makes him more childish than the Otto who had slapped him so many years earlier for leaving his mother. Otto comments 'ya veo como estás' ('I see how you are'), but his father replies 'you've never seen anything, least of all me', echoing Jota's petulant complaint to at Sofía at the end of *La ardilla*.

Ana has become a teacher in her old, now mixed, classroom where she can look across at the Otto's teacher who is now her lover. A child throws a paper plane but there is nothing on it. A sequence of young women come and go in Otto's room and his response to their queries about the woman in the photograph become progressively more detached from the first, that she died of love, to the last, that she died rinsing a lettuce. Ana also goes to Álvaro's but he does not have Otto's address. She tells him her mother wants to go to Australia and looks at the family photo in which Otto holds her note. There are two versions of this photograph, one with the younger and one with the older actors, to suggest that time is irrelevant to significant recollections. Álvaro, as doggedly in denial as his former incarnation, Jota, says if they had behaved like brother and sister the family would still be together.

More dislocated events show Ana arriving at her mothers after leaving Javier, and Álvaro providing the connection with his father in Finland; his oddly, one-dimensional character represents the fact that, like the upward-skiing Finn, he is merely a messenger in this fairytale. Ana is shown in a plane reading a guide to Lapland with another photo of a reindeer, a long shot of another plane passing and a close up of Otto looking up suggest that, like the lovers in *La ardilla*, they are unknowingly passing one another in a way that will be repeated in the later image of the plane passing overhead reflected in Ana's legs in the lake.

A high shot of an old plane is a premonition of Otto's crash, as Otto blows out smoke, indifferent to the film he is watching with his father. He says disaster movies bore him, although, ironically, the film is the fictional recreation of a real plane crash. He finds the letter from Ana with her address in Finland and the declaration she has found 'la casualidad que estábamos esperando' ('the chance they were waiting for'). As he reads her letter that tells the second part of the story he has been told about German Otto, he (Fele Martínez) plays Otto in the flashback and Ana (Najwa Nimri) plays the Spanish women, Cristina, Otto fell in love with.

Ana

Finnish/German Otto tells Ana the love story she has just conveyed to Otto in her letter. He has not been to the cabin since his wife, Cristina died seven years earlier. They discuss their palindromic names and the fact that life is full of mysteries that have no explanation. He says his name is the only German thing he has left and that, on the day Cristina died, his son wrote to say he had fallen in love with a Spaniard (Ana's mother). Ana says she also received a gift that day and the focus cuts to the red leather heart.

At the cabin, she is shot from behind turning as the focus moves from her eyes to the painting of the reindeer on the wall, signed by Cristina and dated 1980, the same year Ana and Otto met. The Arctic Circle is comically painted across the floor and Ana smiles as she pulls her bags inside it. She sees the date and subject of the painting as a premonition but the knock at the door is not her Otto, but Aki who announces he has been sent by Otto. Editing cuts to Ana by lake as the narrative begins to approach its end. Ever superstitious, she tells herself if she runs for the mail van there will be something for her, but the parcel is Olga's video-letter from Sydney. In a parody of communication, Ana answers the gaps left by her mother who seems to apologise. Her comment that she doesn't know where Otto is but he is no doubt up in the clouds, as always, reduces Ana to tears and the screen fades to white.

Alfredo Martínez Expósito notes that the Arctic Circle is another circular metaphor, but that it also marks out the possibility that that the lovers might meet again and that their story might conclude traditionally. He sees Olga, represented here in the video, as the 'negative' of Ana. Instead of Ana's geometric repetitions she has found a geographically opposed end to her story (*53*). Molina Foix notes a similar opposition when he praises Maru Valdiveilso performance 'enviando desde Australia su realidad de telediario a los amantes que viven en la metáfora de las nubes ('sending from Australia her television-news version of reality to the lovers who live in metaphorical clouds') (*34*, p.23).

'El círculo polar' ('The Arctic Circle')

The sound of the plane and the high shot over Finland represent the 'aterrizaje', the coming down to earth of the journey and the story. A close-up of the map shows yet another circle with Ana's name scribbled in it as the focus cuts to the shot of her in the lake with the plane reflected between her legs. The red automatic pilot light blinks and Otto appears, laughing hysterically, apparently having parachuted to land, to borrow Santaolalla's term, at another 'slight angle' from Ana (*57*, p.334). Ana is preparing for the midnight sun which she watches from her white chair by the lake in her white clothes and leather boots. The sun crosses the sky, Ana eats, a reindeer bellows and scratches its head at the bottom of Otto's tree. There is a shot of the rock in the lake and the sun crossing the horizon as the dialogue returns to Otto's comment that life should have circles but his is incomplete. Ana runs to catch the post and hears of the plane crash. Otto shouts helplessly at the red van. The white van passing in the other direction stops and Aki, the personification of the surreal upward skier, helps Otto down. Aki tells him Ana is in the post van and Otto says 'Ana's a messenger like me?', but Aki explains she is only a passenger and they go after her.

'Los ojos de Ana' ('Ana's Eyes')

Ana buys the paper with the photograph of the plane crash that was blowing in the opening moments of the film. She turns looking up at German/Finnish Otto in the window of his flat, and begins to cry as she crosses the road. Editing cuts from her eyes to her legs running up the dark stairway to Otto's flat where she, like Otto in his dead mother's flat, is too scared to look in the kitchen. Otto appears in doorway and they hug, but the focus returns to the close-up of her dying eyes and Otto's reflection.

'Otto en los ojos de Ana' ('Otto in Ana's Eyes')

Otto takes the same journey into town as Ana. Aki puts on the Finnish song to 'ease' Otto's mind. As they approach the newsstand, Aki brakes to avoid the bus that kills Ana. Otto bangs his head and asks, dazed, if Aki knows how to ski upwards as Ana's prone figure shoots in a surreal motion across the screen like a pair of skis. As Otto runs to her, he tightly closes his eyes, as if he might change reality like a camera lens, but he opens them onto the extreme close-up of her eyes with his reflection. The focus zooms closer until his face fills the screen altogether, then disappears to reveal the original shot of the crashed plane and the dedication to Medem's father. Black credits on the white screen are accompanied by the sound of the wind and the haunting, melancholy wind instruments of the Finnish song.

Conclusion

This apparently simple love story masks formal complexities that cannot be fully appreciated from a single viewing. One reviewer criticised the 'fussy academic' double point of view (*32*, p. 92) but this was an exception among the mainly positive responses. Via Rivera was not blinkered by the circles. She notes that all straight lines are just part of a much vaster circle and says the film is 'constructed from beginning to end like a labyrinth' (*62*, p.205). Heredero thought the parents were miscast, but praised the superior structure and script (*39*, p.271). He remarks that this is Medem's most mature and harmonious film to date and describes the story as 'una indagación en los círculos concéntricos formados por dos miradas que se encuentran en el umbral mismo de la muerte' ('an investigation into the concentric circles formed by two gazes that meet at the very edge of death') (*39*, pp.268–269). Vicente Molina Foix, who expressed reservations about *Tierra*, says that few lyrical films match the 'irrompible lógica interna de este vigoroso poema elegíaco' ('indestructible internal logic of this vigorous elegiac poem') (*34*, p.23). Javier Hernández Ruiz mentions the almost mathematical rigour of the narrative and that Medem successfully controls the difficult combination of 'el álgebra narrativa y la poesía' ('the algebraic narrative and the poetry') (*31*, p.30). José Luis Sánchez Noriega praised the representation of the unconscious (*37*, p.19) and Via Rivera notes that 'it is not infinite space that Medem hopes to show, but rather the limitless mazes of the human psyche' (*62*, p.210).

Although Romney suggests the film's geometrical logic implies 'the possibility that everything is simply a formal game generated from abstractions (opposites, doubles, mirror images)' (*36*, p.48), Medem says the lovers invent their own destiny (*44*, p.237). He always envisaged this as a tragic love story that would pay homage to the fact that eternal love exists only in the context of death (*44*, p. 238–89). He says the image of Otto in Ana's eyes 'se quedaré congelado para siempre, retenido en vida en la pupila de su amante muerta' ('will remain frozen for ever, kept alive in the pupil of his dead lover's eye') (*44*, p.239). Otto is caught perpetually in Ana's eye, like an image on film stock.

Santaolalla says that this second generation wave of Basque directors 'seem to be searching for "new" spaces' and formal strategies, expanding territorial and representational limits in order to incorporate "other" settings and stories, allowing themselves to use fabulation and metaphorical discourse, freed now from the burden of political or nationalistic representation' (*57*, p.332). Beck also notes that 'because the elements of Basque identity become more and more liminal in his films the focus of address shifts between the regional and national to a vision of peninsular concerns in relation to globalization' (*46*, p.161). The regional/national divide between Spain and the Basque Country is, as Medem would come to acknowledge in *La pelota vasca*, an inevitable aspect of the work of directors born in the Basque country, but, as he and his peers have also noted, it is not necessarily fundamental. There are many universal themes reflected in Medem's geographical locations. His films have recognisable Basque influences (The Third Carlist War, geographic locations, Basque mythology and place names), but their focus is clearly global.

Conclusion

La pelota vasca: Subjective Points of View

'Secuencia cero'

For my exmination of these four films I have borrowed Medem's term, 'secuencia cero', to refer to the way he uses the opening minutes as a visual lure, drawing the viewer into the film (*44*, p.223). My own 'secuencia cero' to this guide was 'Death Threats and Standing Ovations'. More bluntly melodramatic and far less subtle than Medem's, my own 'secuencia...' hoped to lure the reader in by highlighting the drama of his journey from obscurity to international fame and national notoriety in just over ten years. I would like to return to the source of this controversy, *La pelota vasca*, to sum up the themes I have outlined in his work.

The Auteur *in the Text*

If the definition of an auteur is that his or her films have a signature that is recognisably their own, then Medem is clearly more 'authorial' than most. The sense of mystery he discovered in childhood when he made films with his father's borrowed camera has never left him. For Medem, the mystery lay in the way the camera not only transposed life onto film but transposed something of Medem, the person behind the camera, onto the film image (*3*, p.552). This is the appeal for those who fall on the positive side of the critical divide, the fact that his films convey such an intensely personal impression of both the mundane and the extraordinary in our perception of our lives.

Medem's interest in perception led him towards psychiatry and gave him an insight into the unconscious structures that formulate our thoughts, however, rather than continuing to study these scientifically he chose to represent them on-screen in the formal, poetic structure of his films. Martínez Expósito says:

> El logro de Medem no es menor. Haber conseguido situarse entre los autores más respetados del nuevo cine europeo y haberse forjado un nombre tanto en Euskadi como en los circuitos cinematográficos internacionales, representa toda una hazaña para un director de apenas media docena de películas. Pero haberlo conseguido sin dejar de ser el poeta visual que es, resulta sorprendente y alentador. (*53*).

> Medem's success is no less than this: to have managed to become one of the most respected authors of new European film, to have made a name for himself in the Basque Country and on the international film circuit, is a major feat for someone who has directed only half a dozen films. But to have managed this without ceasing to be a visual poet remains suprising and inspiring.

The formal abstraction intensifies the representation of emotion in Medem's films and they return almost neurotically to the intangible and the irrational. In *Vacas*, it is represented in the zoom through the cow's eye and the focus on the hollow trunk fading to blackness; it is there in the intensity of the editing of the dark night and the waves at the beginning of *La ardilla*; in *Tierra* it is in the fades to the black sky and stars, and in *Los amantes* it is revealed in the fades to white and the repeated narrative returns. Their narrative structure also explores the potential for the violent fragmentation of individual identity, whether as a result of war, in *Vacas*, where the frightened Manuel protects himself by painting his cows, or of a more fundamental kind of terror that motivates Jota to write a song to defend himself in the face of his presumed irrelevance to Sofia in *La ardilla*. Threats to our sense of ourself are also represented in the locations and the forces of nature: the drowned valley in *La ardilla*, the invisible wild boar in *Vacas*, the cosmos from which Ángel is symbolically ejected in *Tierra*, and the eternal sun and arctic landscapes of *Los amantes*. Perhaps this capacity to contemplate and visually represent our precarious psychological foundations lay behind the filming of *La pelota vasca*.

La pelota vasca (2003)

Medem's ability to negotiate multiple points of view led to problems after the premiere of *La pelota vasca*. His laudable aim in making this documentary was to highlight the need for dialogue to put an end to terrorism. It was filmed and edited solely by Medem and is a montage of edited interviews with people whose lives have been affected by ETA. His aim was to give equal time to the views of politicians, victims, and relatives of alleged ETA terrorists. The subject of Basque nationalism was one Medem was finding it increasingly difficult to avoid. His adolescent rebellion against his father had made him emphasize his own maternal Basque roots, and his medical degree led him back to the Basque Country. As he gained prominence in the Spanish film industry, he found himself drawn unwillingly into the regional/national debate. On the release of *Vacas*, he commented openly on Basque nationalism, but by the time *La ardilla roja* was released he was more cautious. Although he says the Basque country is a point of reference, 'es lógico, allí nací y allí vivo' ('it's logical, I was born there and I live there'), he also said that 'por ahora, no estoy interesado en reflejar […] la actual sociedad vasca. Sería demasiado complicado, porque existen muchísimas connotaciones políticas que no me apetece abordar. No quiero provocar malentendidos' ('For now, I'm not interested in reflecting Basque society. It would be too complicated, there are too many political aspects I don't want to go into. I don't want to provoke misunderstandings') (*10*).

Despite his wish to avoid controversy, he was more and more subject to conflicting labels. He was considered 'Basque' (born in the Basque Country) and 'anti-Basque' (for directing films made in Castilian and not Euskera). Fame brought with it the sense that he was becoming an outsider in the place of his birth (San Sebastián) and in the place where he lived (Madrid), as well as being perceived as a potential traitor to both. His response was to make a documentary he hoped would emphasize the dangers of labels and the need for dialogue.

Basque Separatism: Point-of-view/ Points of view

One of the most consistent themes of Medem's fiction films is their sensitive and at times comic understanding of the fragility of human identity and of the need to accommodate and celebrate different points of view. Human identity is never fixed in his films it swings like a pendulum between fluctuating points of view. His intention in *La pelota vasca* was to project a neutral version of the various sides of the political debate over Basque separatism, the role of ETA and the Spanish State. The camera stands in for Medem functioning as a silent interlocutor to the different sides of the debate, but at the same time the film is directed and edited solely by Medem. His own work should have alerted him to the difference between point-of-view filming (from whose point of view the image is perceived) and the point of view of the individuals on whom the lens is focused, and his subtle appreciation of the importance of this should have alerted him to the fact that the camera lens is never neutral. There were violent objections to the way the film gave screen time to people associated with terrorism, as well as enraged disputes and threats of retribution. Medem describes the way such a visceral response to the film affected him: 'me sentí mordido hasta los huesos […]. Y yo apenas me pude mantener de pie, sin apenas responder a tanta agresividad' ('I felt cut to the bone […]. I could hardly stand up, let alone respond to so much aggression') (*44*, p.263–64). Sadly, the film reproduced the violent divisions he hoped it might begin to erase. Although he received standing ovations at its premiere and when he appeared at the Goyas (the Spanish Oscars), he received death threats and was ostracised by a distant member of his own extended family. What *La pelota vasca* revealed, beyond the need for dialogue, was the power of the camera lens to impose extreme emotions onto others: Medem was accused simultaneously of being anti-ETA and pro-ETA and painful though this must have been, Medem had explored similar paradoxes in the four fiction films that led towards this point in his career.

Paradoxical Fictions and Journeys

The paradox arises because our sense of identity derives not only from the way we see ourselves but from the way we are seen by others. Each of Medem's films explores this: from the cow's eye-view in *Vacas*, the squirrel's in *La ardilla*, the cosmic views in *Tierra*, to the alternating points of view of the couple in *Los amantes*. The question of identity in Medem's films is always approached in a way that mixes the trite with the poignant and the banal with the tragic and that is often achieved in the formal mixing of genres. Critics have noted the literary emphasis of the voices-off, dense, wordy dialogues, and the division of *Vacas* and *Los amantes* into sections with different headings (*44*, p.74). Medem also fills his films 'with narrative complexities and structural non-sequiturs that break both genre conventions and the cause-and-effect logic of a linear narrative' (*46*, p.150). They move from black comedy to tragedy in the blink of an eye, and perhaps cut the ground from beneath viewers who would like to categorise them more easily. Content and form are fused, narrative continuity and realism are suppressed in favour of the oneiric and poetic, so that cinematography, *mise-en-scène*, *diegesis*, and point of view combine to reinforce the recurring themes of national identity, love, war, and the gender-divide all of which are projected onto natural or urban landscapes that gently expose the grandiose pretensions and all-too human fallibility of his characters.

Medem describes the making of each film as a journey from which he feels he never wholly returns and that leaves a vacancy, or sense of loss, that motivates the next film 'pues una parte de ti se queda para siempre allí. Y vuelves con un agujero inmenso que tienes que rellenar otra vez' ('because a part of you remains behind and you come back with a huge hole you have to fill again') (*27*).

This comment may explain the way his film resonate one with the next. Stone notes the topic of cowardice is transferred from the beginning and end of *Vacas* to the opening sequences of *La ardilla*, and Heredero wonders whether the drowning Carmelo Gómez at the end of *La ardilla* might be read into Ángel, also played by Carmelo Gómez, in *Tierra*, who has died and come back to life (*61*, p.167; *3*, pp.575–77). Others have noted the recurring theme of escape in his work and of journeys that 'can be read as the fictional parallels of Medem's own creative quest' (*58*, p.312). The locations of his first four features have moved further and further outwards to the edge of the Arctic Circle in a way that suggests Medem may have wanted to disassociate himself from the problems of the Basque Country, and yet all of them continue to debate individual, regional or national identity in a way Santaolalla evocatively describes: 'like Trojan horses, Medem's constructs conceal hidden forces raging with turmoil and dissidence, ready to unsettle complacent notions of individual and national identity' (*58*, p. 312).

Visual Lift-Off and 'aterrizajes'

Whatever their ultimate trajectory, Medem's films begin with a single image, for example, a woodcutter flinging an axe into a forest, and the writing of the screenplay evolves from this point. It is because of the dominance of the visual over the narrative that it is possible to watch his films and interpret their endings in different ways. The initial visual image is one Medem tries not to analyse too much in case he deprives it of its force (*44*, p. 69) and for the same reason, unlike other directors, he rarely used a storyboard in the making of these four films except in the case of the digitalised sequences in *Tierra* (*44*, p. 73). He says:

> En el arranque de mis películas intento mostrar el lugar por donde se tiene que entrar en ellas, trato de enseñar cuáles son las reglas y los códigos de la historia, para que, una vez dentro, no exista esa diferenciación entre la imagen conmovida y la imagen narrativa. (*3*, p.565)
>
> From the beginning of my films I try to show viewers the way in, I try to teach them the rules and codes of the narrative, so that once they are inside, there is no difference between the emotional and narrative imagery.

Like Víctor Erice, the Spanish director who impressed Medem so profoundly when saw *El espíritu de la colmena* at the age of seventeen, Medem is interested in new ways of creating meaning on-screen. Although the stories his films tell are important, what makes them stand out are the formal and aesthetic structures that 'tell' them (*15*, p. 81). Medem explores the fantastic without ever quite leaving the realms of the real. This is because he recognises the 'real' to be something we never fully comprehend, so his characters function in a world we recognize as well as in one we may not, and his films combine the cerebral with the visceral in a way that allows their complex narratives to remain accessible, leading us on a visual, intellectual and emotional journey, then bringing us gently back down to earth.

Select Cast, Crew and Awards

Vacas (1992)

Emma Suárez (Cristina), Carmelo Gómez (Manuel / Ignacio / Peru), Ana Torrent (Catalina), Karra Elejalde (llegorri / Lucas), Klara Badiola (Madalem), Txema Blasco (Manuel), Kándido Uranga (Carmelo / Juan), Pilar Bardem (Paulina), Miguel Ángel García (Peru child), Ane Sánchez (Cristina child), Magdalena Mikolajczyk (eldest daughter, child), Enara Azkue (middle daughter, child), Ortzi Balda (Ilegorri child / Lucas child), Elisabeth Ruiz (eldest sister), Ramón Barea (judge), Aitor Mazo (soldier 1), Xabier Aldanondo (soldier 2), Carlos Zabala (officer), Antxón Echeverría (Carlist 1), Alberto Arizaga (Carlist 2), Niko Lizeaga (Carlist 3), Patxi Santamaría (Reporter 1), José Ramón Soriz (Reporter 2)

Production: *Sogetel* in partnership with *Idea, S.A.*, also subsidised by the *ICAA* (Spanish Ministry of Culture) and Cultural Department of the Basque Government
Executive Producers: José Luis Olaizola, Fernando Garcillán
Screenplay: Julio Medem, Michel Gaztambide
Editing: María Elena Saiz de Rozas
Artistic Director: Rafael Palmero
Director of photography: Carles Gusi
Music: Alberto Iglesias
Laboratory: Fotofilm Madrid, S.A.
Locations: Valle de Baztán, Señorío de Bertiz (Navarra)
Special Effects: Reyes Abades
Duration: 93 minutes

Goya Award for 'Best New Director', 1993; Turin Festival Prize for 'Best Film', 1992; 'Gold Prize for New Directors', Tokyo International Film Festival, 1992; 'Best Film' and 'Best Cinematography' (Charles Gusi), Alexandria Film Festival, 1993; 'Special Prize for Best First Feature', Montreal Festival, 1992; 'Sutherland Prize', British Film Institute, 1993; 'Jury Prize', Beauvais Festival, Francia, 1994; Sant Jordi Critics' Prize for 'Best First Feature', Barcelona, 1993; 'Cid Prize', Burgos Festival 1992; 'Best First Feature', Ecological Film Festival, Tenerife, 1992; 'Best

Screenplay', CEC (Cinema Writers' Circle), Madrid, 1993; 'Best Actor' (Carmelo Gómez), Spanish Actors' Union, 1993; 'Best New Director', 'Best Script' (Julio Medem and Michel Gaztambide), 'Best Soundtrack' (Alberto Iglesias), 'Best Basque Actor' (Txema Blasco), 'Best Basque Actress' (Klara Badiola), World of Basque Film, 1992; 'Icarus Prize for Young Directors', *Diario 16*, 1992; 'Special Prize', *ICAA*, Spanish Ministry of Culture, 1994

La ardilla roja (1993)

Emma Suárez (Lisa / Sofía), Nancho Novo (Jota), María Barranco (Carmen), Karra Elejalde (Antón), Carmelo Gómez (Félix), Elena Irureta (Begoña), Susana García (Eli), Ane Sánchez (Cristina), Eneko Irizar (Alberto), Sarai Noceda (Ana), Maite Yerro (Nicola), Txema Blasco (Chief Neurologist), Chete Lera (Salvador), Gustavo Salmerón (Luis Alfonso), Susana Hernádez (Doctor), José Ma Sacristán (Doctor), Andreas Prittwitz (Otto).

Production: *Sogetel, S.A.*, also subsidised by the Ministery of Culture
Executive Producer: Fernando Garcillán
Production Manager: Ricardo García Arrojo.
Screenplay: Julio Medem
Director of Photography: Gonzalo Fernández Berridi
Editing: María Elena Sainz de Rozas
Music: Alberto Iglesias
Laboratory: Madrid Films
Songs: 'Elisa' and '*La ardilla roja*', written by Julio Medem, performed by Txetxo Bengoetxea, 'Let There Be Love', written by James Grant, performed by Nat King, *Der Freischütz*, 'Ännchen's Aria', Carl Maria von Weber.
Locations: San Sebastián, San Martín de Valdeiglesias, Pelayos de la Presa, Usanos, Valsain, El Pardo, Madrid
Duration: 114 minutes

Goya Award for 'Best Original Music' (Alberto Iglesias), 1994; 'Youth Prize' and 'Public Prize for Best Foreign Film', Cannes 1993; 'Gold Precolombian Circle Prize', Internacional Film Festival, Bogota 1994; 'Special Jury Prize' and 'Critic's Prize', Fantasy Film Festival Gerardmer (Francia) 1994; 'Golden Palm Award', Independent Cinema Festival Eanderdale (USA), 1994; 'Special Director's Priz', International Film Festival, Denver (USA), 1993; Sant Jordi Critic's Prize for 'Best Spanish Film' and 'Best Spanish Actress' (Emma Suárez), 1993; Actor's Union Prizes for 'Best Actress' (Emma Suárez) and 'Best Actor' (Nancho Novo), 1994; Basque World of Film Prize for 'Best Film', 'Best Director', 'Best Music' (Alberto Iglesias), 'Best Basque Actress' (Ane Sánchez); 'Luis

Buñuel Prize for Best Film of the Year', *Positif* (France), 1994; 'Best Film' and 'Best Screenplay', Young Film Festival, Bucarest (Rumania), 1995.

Tierra (1996)

Carmelo Gómez (Ángel), Emma Suárez (Ángela), Karra Elejalde (Patricio), Silke (Mari), Nancho Novo (Alberto), Txema Blasco (Tomás), Ane Sánchez (Ángela daughter), Juan José Suárez "Paquete" (Manuel), Ricardo Amador (Charly), César Vea (Mildo), Pepe Viyuela (Ulloa), Alicia Agut (Cristina), Miguel Palenzuela (Ángel's uncle), Vicente Haro (Mayor), Adelfina Serrano (Concha), José Amador (Tony), Montse García Romeu (Mildo's wife).

Production: *Sogetel, S.A.* and *Lola Films, S.A.*, in collaboration with *Sogepaq, S.A.*, and in association with *Canal +*
Producer: Fernando Garcillán
Screenplay: Julio Medem
Director of Photography: Javier Aguirresarobe
Editing: Iván Aledo
Artistic Director: Satur Idarret
Music: Alberto Iglesias
Songs: '*Tierra*' by Caetano Veloso; 'Túmbala si puedes' by Barbería del Sur; 'Izar ederra' by Ruper Ordorika; 'Sólo para locos' by Marc Parrot; 'Baile del tractor', composed by Gaby Pereira
Locations: Cariñena, Cosuenda, Paniza, Calatayud (Zaragoza), Funes (Navarra), Peñíscola (Castellón)
Duration: 125 minutes

Goya Awards for 'Best Original Music' (Alberto Iglesias) and 'Best Special Effects' (Reyes Abades and Ignacio Sanz Pastor), 1997; 'Special Jury Prize', Sao Paulo Internacional Film Festival (Brazil), 1997; 'Best Film', 'Best Director', 'Best Cinematography' (Javier Aguirresarobe), 'Best Artistic Director' (Satur Idarreta), Basque World of Film, 1996; Meliá-Olid Prize for 'Best Spanish Film', 'Best Director' and 'Best Actor' (Carmelo Gómez), 1996; 'San Pancracio Prize for Best Director of the Year', *Versión Original* (Cáceres); 'Best Spanish Film of the Year', *Cartelera Turia* (Valencia).

Los Amantes del Círculo Polar (1998)

Nawja Nimri (Ana), Fele Martínez (Otto), Nancho Novo (Álvaro), Maru Valdivielso (Olga), Peru Medem (Otto child), Sara Valiente (Ana child), Víctor Hugo Oliveira (Otto teenager), Kristel Díaz (Ana teenager), Pep Munné (Otto's teacher), Jaroslaw Bielski (Álvaro Midelman), Rosa Morales

(Ana's teacher), Joost Siedhoff (Otto Midelman), Beate Jensen (Otto's mother), Petri Heino (Aki).

Production: Alicia Produce and Bailando en la Luna for Sogetel, in collaboration with Canal +, Sogepaq and Le Studio Canal
Producers: Fernando Bovaira, Enrique López Lavigne
Executive Producers: Txarli Llorente, Fernando de Garcillán
Screenplay: Julio Medem
Director of Photography: Gonzalo F. Berridi
Editing: Ivan Aledo
Artistic Direction: Sadur Idarreta, Karmele Soler, Estibalitz Markiegi, Itziar Arrieta
Music: Alberto Iglesias
Locations: Madrid, Helsinki, Rovaniemi (Finland)
Duration: 112 minutes

Goya Award for 'Best Original Music' (Alberto Iglesias) and 'Best Editing' (Ivan Aledo) 1998; 'Best European Film', Brussels Festival, 1999, 'Best Film', University Jury, Festival at Toulouse, 1998; 'Public Prize for Best Latin Film', 'Best Director' and 'Critics' Prize', Gramado Film Festival; Onda Prizes for 'Best Spanish Film' and 'Best Actress' (Najwa Nimri)

Bibliography

A: INTERVIEWS WITH JULIO MEDEM

1. Apaoloza, Jon, '*Tierra* tiene algo más de mí que mis anteriores películas', *Sur de Málaga*, 'Cine', 2 June 1996, 15. Medem defines film-making as a form of therapy, and says he is unlikely to move to Hollywood.
2. Castro, Antonio, *Dirigido*, 247 (June 1996), 66–69. Discussion of making and meaning of *Tierra*.
3. Heredero, Carlos F., 'Julio Medem: La imagen conmovida', in *Espejo de miradas. Entrevistas con nuevos directores del cine español de los años noventa* (Alcalá de Henares: Edición del Festival de Cine de Alcalá de Henares /Ayuntamiento de Alcalá de Henares-Fundación Colegio del Rey/ C.A.M., 1997), pp.547–87. Extremely useful interview discussing the influence of Bergman and Erice, Medem's fascination with the unconscious and the theme of the natural landscape.
4. Hernández, Esteban, *El mundo* (Madrid), 'Cultura', 26 April 1993, 55. Joint interview with directors Bajo Ulloa and Marc Recha, in which Medem says 'yo nunca quiero colocarme racionalmente en ningún sitio' and that the writing process is always 'más puro' than the finished product.
5. Smith, Paul Julian, 'Angels to Earth', *Sight and Sound*, 7.8 (August 1997), 12–14. Very astute analysis of the film and useful interview with Medem.

B: PRESS ARTICLES ON MEDEM

6. Arenas, José, 'No dirigí *El Zorro* con Spielberg porque no me gustan los filmes de encargo', ABC (Madrid), 'Espectáculos', 19 March 1997, 80. Medem on Mari's diary and the fact that his films have found a wider audience internationally than in Spain.
7. Arenas, José, 'No se ha reflejado en la prensa el éxito de *Tierra* en Cannes', ABC (Madrid), 'Espectáculos', 22 May 1996, 89. Describes Medem as one of the Spanish directors 'con más tirón' and corrects negative reports in the Spanish press about reception of *Tierra* at Cannes.

8. García, Eva, 'Quiero conmover al espectador', *El periódico* (Zaragoza), 3 September 1998. Medem discusses casting and *Los amantes*, saying the notion of eternal love is a 'limit', a quiet place with no future. He notes the various circles in the film change according to the point of view and the way the two protagonists put a 'secret bubble' around themselves into which the viewer is invited.

9. García, Rocío, '*Tierra* nació del alma', *El país* (Madrid), 'La Cultura', 9 May 1996, 37. Medem explains Ángel's anxiety and defines the film as 'una reflexión antimística y con un mensaje antitrascendental'.

10. Gutiérrez, Isabel, '*Vacas* es mi rival más duro, el más peligroso', *Blanco y negro* (Madrid), sección Agenda, 25 April 1993. Discussion of *La ardilla*.

11. Martín-Lunas, Milagros, 'Julio Medem representará al cine español en Venecia', *El mundo de Madrid* (Madrid), 'Cultura', 16 July 1998, 45. Cites Medem's comment that *Los amantes* 'es una historia de amor en estado puro' and his most direct film so far.

12. Sánchez, Ángel, 'El retrato: Julio Medem', *El periódico Catalunya*, 'Opinión', 26 August 2001. Cites Medem's comment on left-wing politics and the armed struggle in the Basque Country.

13. Zaragoza, J.A.G., 'Julio Medem prepara su nuevo filme, *Tierra*', *Heraldo de Aragón*, 'Espectáculos' (Zaragoza), 6 May 1994, 42.

C: REVIEWS OF FILMS

VACAS

14. Cerdán, Josetxo, in *Antología crítica del cine español. 1906–1995*, ed. Julio Pérez Perucha (Madrid: Catedra/ Filmoteca Española, 1997), pp. 921–23. Extremely detailed discussion noting the influence of Vicente Ameztoy's exhibition *Karne y klorofila*, and the financial restraints that cut the script. Links the film to aesthetic traditions from Picasso, El Greco, Goya and Zuloaga, as well as noting the debt to Borau's *Furtivos* (1975).

15. César, Samuel R., *Dirigido*, 201 (April 1992), 81–82. Positive review emphasising the dominance of imagery over narrative and dialogue 'como en obras de grandes maestros' (81).

16. Martínez Montalbán, *Reseña*, 228 (May 1992), 14. Cautious response to a new director.

17. Vidal, Nuria, *Fotogramas* (May 1992), p.8. Positive analysis highlighting the ancient imagery of the 'enchanted wood' and praising the originality. Also suggests an implied English pun on 'cow' and 'coward'.

18. Yates, Robert, '*Vacas*', *Sight and Sound*, 3.7 (July 1993), 54–55. Notes the connections with fairytales, the dark depiction of reality and Manuel's paintings as a way of taking control.

LA ARDILLA ROJA

19. Besas, Paul, *Variety*, 10 May 1993. Negative, found the men unappealing and the film a 'total letdown'.

20. Kohn, Olivier, *Positif*, 389–390 (July–August 1993), 49. Positive response noting the playful, surreal humour, satirical approach to 'machismo' and the mysteries of femininity.

21. Rouyer, Philippe, *Positif*, 398 (April 1994), 52–53. Links to a Spanish 'New Wave' of comic melodramas by Bigas Luna and Almodóvar, and discusses the mixing of lies and truth and the 'retour grand-guignolesque' of Félix (52). Discusses the linking of the squirrel to the male and female characters.

22. Smith, Paul Julian, *Sight and Sound*, 4.10 (October 1994), 34. Praises the opening, mentions links with *Vertigo*, and says the film 'confirms Medem's place as one of the most original and distinctive directors working in Europe today'.

TIERRA

23. Albert, Antonio, *Cinemanía*, 7 (April 1996), 76–77. Detailed review highlighting the film's poetic qualities.

24. Camiña, Ángel, *Reseña*, 274 (July–August 1996), 3.

25. Elley, Derek, *Variety*, 27 May 1996. Very funny, very negative response.

26. Fernández Valentí, Tomás, *Dirigido*, 246 (May 1996), 50–51.

27. Rivera, Alfonso, 'En *Tierra* de Medem', *El país de las tentaciones*, 27 January 1995, 16. Notes the interest from Kubrick and Spielberg. Cites Medem as a polemical director and quotes him on film-making as a journey, waiting for Banderas, saying *Tierra* is his most autobiographical film, and on the fact that his films are driven by passion.

28. Romney, Jonathan, '*Tierra*', *Sight and Sound*, 7.8 (August 1997), 56. Useful and detailed review, linking Medem with Raúl Ruiz in the pursuit of 'mystification [as] an unqualified virtue'. Notes links to David Lynch and Kie lowski and the references to *La ardilla* in the 'ever-shifting narrative quicksand'.

29. Rouyer, Philippe, *Positif*, 426 (July–August 1996), 131. Notes the return to the theme of the 'double', and praises the cinematography, but finds the film less subtle than *La ardilla* and is critical of the angel's voice off.

30. Sánchez Costa, J.J., 'Julio Medem: '*Tierra* es un viaje de lo complejo a lo sencillo', *El periódico* (Barcelona), 23 May 1996. Cautious response, cites Medem contradicting Spanish press reports of a lukewarm reception at Cannes and his advice to viewers: 'Recomiendo que nadie se complique la vida, sino que todos se dispongan a disfrutar con la mente en blanco' and his description of the film as 'un viaje de lo complejo a lo sencillo'. Notes Medem's love of speed and motorbikes and his delight at the description of *Tierra* as 'un *western* metafísico'.

LOS AMANTES DEL CIRCULO POLAR

31. Hernández Ruiz, Javier, Dirigido, 271 (September 1998), 30–33. Positive response with useful comments on themes and structure.

32. J.L., *Cahiers du Cinéma*, 534 (April 1999), 92. Negative response linking magical element of the love story to Henry Hathaway's *Peter Ibbetson* and the *mise en scène* to films by Jaco Van Dormael, finds the dual point of view 'ne parvient pas à dissimuler un académisme à l'européenne aux image pieuses et mièvres' ('does not manage to disguise a European academic tendency towards pious and vapid imagery').

33. M. B., *Positif*, 459 (May 1999), 46. Emphasises the role of the breakdown of the family in the lovers' passion.

34. Molina Foix, Vicente, *Cinemanía*, 36 (September 1998), 22–23. Positive response noting the loss of symbolic and real fathers in the film and the theme of the natural world also found in *Vacas*. Praises highly the poetic structure and lightly comic touch.

35. Ocaña, Javier, Cinemanía, 36, (September 1998), 82–83. Quotes actors' responses to the script and sources Ray Loriga.

36. Romney, Jonathan, *Sight and Sound*, 10.2 (February 2000), 48. Intelligent, lucid review discussing actors, themes, structure and noting the games of oppositions and multilingual puns (finish/Finnish; the Spanish word *aquí*, and the Finnish name Aki).

37. Sánchez Noriega, José Luis, *Cine para leer*, 298 (October 1998), 19. Very positive, particularly with regard to the represention of the unconscious and poetic qualities, but questions the inclusion of reference to the bombing of Guernica in the sequence with the siblings.

D: WORKS CONTAINING DISCUSSION OF MEDEM

38. Allinson, Mark and Barry Jordan, *Spanish Cinema: A Student's Guide* (London: Hodder Arnold, 2005). Very useful introduction to studying film in general and Spanish film in particular, with discussion of cinematography in *La ardilla* (pp.47–48) and representation in *Vacas* (pp.149–52).

39. Heredero, Carlos F., *20 nuevos directores del cine español* (Madrid: Alianza 1999), pp.248–74. Extended and extremely useful version of the introduction published in 1997 (*3*). Provides detail about Medem's family and life, and intelligent critical analysis of the films

40. Herráez Cubino, Lola, in *Jóvenes realizadores del cine español*, ed. Javier Gutiérrez Martínez (Salamanca: Caja Salamanca y Soria, 1997), pp.56–66. Succinct, impressionistic introduction to these four films with useful, although unsourced, quotation from Medem.

41. Jordan, Barry and Riki Morgan-Tamosunas, *Contemporary Spanish Cinema* (Manchester: Manchester University Press, 1998). Insightful mention of Medem, the rural genre and 'Basqueness' in the 1990s in relation *Vacas* (p.50). Intelligent commentary on *La ardilla* as a psychological thriller (p.101), and on *Tierra* (pp.196–97).

42. Perriam, Chris, *Stars and masculinities in Spanish Cinema: From Banderas to Bardem*, New York: Oxford University Press, 2003). Excellent monograph on Spanish stars, with very useful reference to actor Carmelo Gómez.

43. Triana-Toribio, Nuria, *Spanish National Cinema* (London and New York: Routledge, 2003). A key text for anyone interested in Spanish film. Path-breaking study of the development of film in Spain from the late nineteenth century to the turn of this century.

E: BOOKS ON MEDEM

44. Angulo, Jesús, and José Luis Rebordinos, *Contra la certeza. El cine de Julio Medem* (Huesca: Festival de Cine de Huesca, Filmoteca Vasca, 2004). A key text. Intelligent and detailed analysis of films from the early shorts to *La pelota vasca*. Extremely helpful detail on background and production, informative interviews with Medem and a detailed bibliography.

45. Stone, Rob, *Julio Medem* (Manchester and New York: Manchester University Press, 2007). In press at the time of writing, this will be the key English-language text on Medem. Extremely interesting study combining material from extensive interviews with Medem and other members of crew and cast with insightful analysis of the films.

F: BOOK CHAPTERS / ARTICLES ON MEDEM

46. Beck Jay, 'Mediating the Transitional in Contemporary Spanish Cinema: Pedro Almodóvar and Julio Medem', *Torre de papel*, 10.1 (Spring 2000), 134–69. Detailed updating of Kinder's notion of 'transcultural reinscription' examining the representation of Spanish identity in Almodóvar and Medem. Useful discussion of funding in the Transition period and of the generic hybrid as a means to negotiate the international market. Very useful analysis of point of view in Medem and of his works increasingly liminal locations.

47. Davies, Ann, 'Roads to Nowhere: How Basque Terrorists Cross Space and Place in Cinema', *Bulletin of Hispanic Studies*, 82 (2005), 343–55. Although not on Medem, an interesting examination in relation to *Tierra* of the representation of ETA, national identity and the landscape in Basque film via the motif of the road.
48. De Ros, Xon, '*Vacas* and Basque Cinema: The Making of a Tradition', *Journal of the Institute for Romance Studies*, 5 (1997), 225–354. Illuminating examination of the film and its precursors with reference to film, painting and photography. Essential reading for a wider understanding of the regional context and the metaphorical complexities of the film.
49. Evans, Jo, '*La ardilla roja*: the Compulsive Nostalgia of Popular Love Songs', in *Cultura Popular: Studies in Spanish and Latin American Popular Culture*, eds Shelley Godsland and Anne M. White (Oxford: Peter Lang, 2002), pp.147–162. Analysis of the role of the love songs in the representation of masculinity.
50. Evans, Jo, '*La madre muerta* (1993) and *Tierra* (1995): Basque Identity, or just the Other?', *Studies in European Cinema*, 4.3 (2006), 173–83. Analysis of the representation in these two films in relation to questions of regional identity with reference to Lacan.
51. Gabilondo, Joseba, 'Uncanny Identity: Violence, Gaze, and Desire in Contemporary Basque Cinema', in *Constructing Identity in Contemporary Spain*, ed. Jo Labanyi (Oxford: Oxford University Press, 2002), pp.262–72. Very interesting article using Lacanian psychoanalytic theory in the analysis of the representation of national identity and violence in Basque film.
52. García Sánchez, José M., 'Reinscripción de la tragedia y de la figura femenina en *Los amantes del círculo polar* de Julio Medem', *Espéculo: Revista de Estudios Literarios*, 26 (March 2004), http://www.ucm.es/info/especulo/numero26/medem.html (accessed 17 November 2006). Discusses the flight of the women from traditional roles and displacement of the nuclear family with reference to the traditions of melodrama.
53. Martínez Expósito, Alfredo, 'Julio Medem y la poética del compromiso', *Alpha Revista de Artes, Letras y Filosofía*, 20 (December 2004), 121–34, http://www.scielo.cl/scielo.php?script=sci_arttext&pid=S071822012004000200008&lng=en&nrm=iso&tlng=es (accessed 10 December 2006). Notes the links to Kie lowski's *La double vie de Véronique* (1991) and *Trois couleurs: Rouge* (1994) and provides detailed examination of coincidences in the narrative. Links to Roland Barthes the fact that the viewer has actively to engage in creating meaning in

the film, and with Ortega y Gasset the use of formal abstraction to convey emotion.

54. Richardson, Nathan E., 'Animals, Machines, and Postnational Identity in Julio Medem's *Vacas*', *Tesserae: Journal of Iberian and Latin American Studies*, 10.2 (Fall 2002), 191–204. Lucid, thought-provoking examination of the film in relation to cyborg theory (mistakes Carmelo for an 'Irigibel' on p.195).

55. Rodríguez, María Pilar, Ch.2, 'Genealogías violentas y exilios pasionales: *Vacas* y *Los amantes del Círculo Polar* de Julio Medem', in *Mundos en conflicto: Aproximaciones al cine vasco de los noventa* (San Sebastián: Universidad de Deusto, 2002), pp.75–102. Detailed, wide-ranging discussion including reference to the thematic and formal role of subjectivity in these two films and how their self-reflexity echoes postmodern, fluctuating notions of identity.

56. Sánchez, Antonio, 'Women Immune to a Nervous Breakdown: the Representation of Women in Julio Medem's Films', *Tesserae: Journal of Iberian and Latin American Studies*, 3.2 (1997), 147–61. Perspicacious analysis of the changing representation of gender in *Vacas* and *La ardilla.*

57. Santaolalla, I. C., 'Far From Home, Close to Desire: Julio Medem's Landscapes', BHS, LXXV (1998), 331–337. Extremely useful examination of *Vacas*, *La ardilla* and *Tierra* analysing the motif of the journey with reference to Medem's translation of regional elements across national borders and onto universal themes.

58. Santaolalla, Isabel, C., 'Julio Medem's *Vacas* (1991): Historicizing the Forest', in *Spanish Cinema: The Auteurist Tradition*, ed. Peter Evans (Oxford: Oxford University Press, 1999), pp.310–324. Important essay considering the second generation of Basque directors with reference to Caro Baroja's account of Basque history. Includes discussion of Basque mythology relating 'adur', the feminine principle to the cows and woods, and the axe to its masculine counterpart 'indur', concluding that the theme of rivalry relates not only to the Basque Country, but to the theme of gender division.

59. Smith, Paul Julian, 'Between Heaven and Earth: Grounding Julio Medem's *Tierra*', *BHS* (1999), LXXVI, 11–25. Detailed reading with reference to 'basqueness' and in defence of the film's anti-mysticism.

60. Smith, Paul Julian, 'Julio Medem's *La ardilla roja*: a transparent Society, in *Vision Machines: Cinema, Literature and Sexuality in Spain and Cuba, 1983–1993* (London & New York: Verso, 1996), pp. 128–45. Fascinating analysis via Italian postmodern theorist Vattimo.

61. Stone, Rob, Ch. 8, 'Projections of Desire', in *Spanish Cinema* (Harlow: Pearson, 2002), pp.158–182. Before the publication of (*45*) this was the most detailed study available in English. It provides an extremely detailed and accessible introduction to Medem and the films up to *Los amantes*.

62. Via Rivera, Marian, 'A Journey into the Labyrinth: Intertextual Readings of Borges and Cortázar in Julio Medem's *Los amantes del círculo polar* (1998)', *Tesserae: Journal of Iberian and Latin American Studies*, 10.2 (Dec 2004), 205–12. Subtle and wide-ranging analysis of the role of superstition, the labyrinth and games in the film with reference to Bonitzer, Cortázar and Borges.
63. White, Anne M., 'Manchas blancas, manchas negras', in *Spanish Cinema: Calling the Shots*, eds Rob Rix and Roberto Rodríguez-Saona (Leeds: Trinity and All Saints, 1999), pp.1–14. Very lucid analysis of the film with particular reference to the representation of the patriarchal desire for reproduction.
64. Yraola, Aitor, 'El discurso de la muerte en *Vacas* de Julio Medem', in *Cine-Lit: Essays on Hispanic Film and Fiction*, eds George Cabello-Castellet, Jaume Martí Olivella & Guy H. Woods (Portland: Portland State University, 1995), pp.163–68. Analysis of the theme of death in *Vacas*, with useful synopsis (Manuel cited as the 'nuevo aizcolari' instead of Ignacio on p.166).

G: SCREENPLAYS BY JULIO MEDEM

65. Medem, Julio, *Tierra / Mari en la Tierra (Diario de un personaje)* (Barcelona: Planeta, 1997)
66. Medem, Julio, *Los amantes del Círculo Polar* (Madrid: Alta Films, 1998)
67. Medem, Julio, *Lucía y el sexo* (Madrid: Ocho y Medio, 2001)
68. Medem, Julio, *La pelota vasca. La piel contra la piedra* (Madrid: Aguilar, 2003)